THE WHOLEMEAL MICROBAKE BOOK

HEALTH
RIGHT

THE WHOLEMEAL MICROBAKE BOOK

JANETTE MARSHALL

J. M. DENT & SONS LTD
London

First published 1988
© Janette Marshall, 1988

This book is set in 11/12 Linotron Goudy by
Gee Graphics Ltd
Made in Great Britain by
Butler & Tanner, Frome and London for
J. M. Dent & Sons Ltd
91 Clapham High Street, London SW4 7TA

British Library Cataloguing in Publication Data

Marshall, Janette
  The wholemeal microbake book.
  1. Microwave cookery 2. Baking
  I. Title
  641.7'1   TX832

ISBN 0-460-12540-0

Contents

Introduction – Why Microbake?

Hello and welcome to *The Wholemeal Microbake Book*. I am tempted to say,

> If I'd known you were coming
> I'd have baked a cake.

If it were possible to give you a taste of the goodies this book has to offer I am sure you would be hooked at once, but instead I shall have to tickle your tastebuds with the written word.

Perhaps I could start by explaining 'microbake'. It is a word I devised specially when writing this book, to represent an entirely new departure in microwave cookery. *The Wholemeal Microbake Book* demonstrates to the full the possibilities for baking authentically and deliciously using your microwave oven.

This has been a sadly neglected area, since microwave baking using conventional ingredients produces pale and uninteresting cakes and biscuits, pies and pastries. The wholemeal microbake approach introduces a new and exciting dimension, giving not only healthier recipes, but also better results – due in part to the naturally rich colours and textures of wholemeal or unrefined ingredients, and in part to the imaginative use of decorations and glazes to add to the mouthwatering appearance.

This book also aims to help you make more of the diversity and versatility of baked food, which is a significant part of the diet for most of us. Nearly everyone eats some baked items each day, be it toast for breakfast, biscuits for elevenses, bread in sandwiches for lunch, or pies and flans for main courses, and puddings at dinner. Many of these we buy, because we simply don't have the time to bake them ourselves, even if we do get pleasure from the smell of home baking, and the satisfaction of creating something ourselves and seeing others enjoy the food we have made for them.

The Wholemeal Microbake Book can, through the new technology of microwave cooking, bring back some of the old-fashioned traditional joys of home baking, but without the long waiting. Because the recipes are all devised with health in mind, they will also help to change your own and your family's eating habits for the better. Instead of using the refined white flour and other products that are often high in salt and sugar, you will now be able to make high-fibre, low-sugar and even salt-free versions of favourite dishes in a fraction of the time that it would normally take. And if you have never tried home baking, the speed and efficiency of the microwave, together with its cleanliness, might just persuade you to start something new that you will find both rewarding and fun.

There is no need to worry, either, if you find microbaking becomes something of an addiction because it is one of those rare hobbies that will actually save you money. A microwave oven runs off a 13 amp plug, so it is much cheaper than a conventional oven, and because it cooks so quickly it uses less electricity. Microbaking is also energy-saving in that microwave ovens are 40 per cent efficient compared with 14 per cent for electric ovens and 7 per cent for gas (efficiency is the ratio of energy utilized to energy actually given out by the appliance.) Baking brownies from scratch, for example, will take nearly 1 kilowatt per hour in a conventional oven compared with 0.17 kilowatts in a microwave.

Homemade items using the high-quality 'healthy' ingredients recommended in this book are also, of course, much cheaper in other ways than the shop versions – and you would be hard put to find many of these recipes in the shops at all.

Whichever way you look at it, with *The Wholemeal Microbake Book* you just can't lose.

Wholemeal Microbaking

The Wholemeal Microbake Book meets a longstanding need, because most microwave cookery books have consistently ignored the potential of this area. Either they have dismissed microbaked items as pale and insipid, needing lots of icing or similar 'tasteless' decoration in order to be acceptable, or they have included a very small selection of easy items that you have probably already worked out how to make for yourself, such as chocolate cake, ginger parkin, flapjacks and a fruit loaf.

The reason most authors avoid microbaked goods is partly because in general they are concerned with a far wider area of microwave cooking than just baking, and partly – as we have already discussed – because they are using the wrong ingredients for the job. White flour and sugar and other refined ingredients are lacking in colour (as well as nutrients), and as microwaving is so quick there is no time for the usual caramelization process that occurs during conventional cooking to brown the food. However, by using wholemeal flour, brown sugars and honey, date syrup and molasses, rich dark dried fruit, and other tasty unrefined ingredients, it is possible to add natural colour to cakes and pastries, biscuits and buns, and bring them nearer to the conventional appearance.

In addition, wholemeal microbaked items will not only be more nutritious but will also have a better flavour than those made from refined ingredients. Since caramelization contributes to flavour as well as appearance, the richer taste of unrefined ingredients is all-important when there is no time for this process to take place.

The Fast Way to Healthier Baking

How often have you been put off baking after you have added up the preparation time, that needed to assemble the ingredients and combine them, the time it takes for the oven to heat up, and the cooking time, and realized that you will either be in bed by the time the cake is due to come out of the oven or that you can go to the late-night convenience store and home again in half the time? That is a shame, because baking is both a creative and a relaxing pastime. It is very satisfying to bake something for yourself or your family and friends – and even more enjoyable to eat it. With microbaking you can respond to an impulse to do some baking and know that the results will be ready in about a third of the time taken by conventional cooking.

There are other time savings, too. Not only do you not have to wait for the oven to heat up, but you don't have to spend ages scouring baked-on grime in the oven or in tins either. Microwave dishes and the microwave oven are both far easier and far quicker to clean. If you opt for a combination oven that combines microwaves with conventional heat you may have a slightly dirtier oven to contend with, and while the products of combination microbaking look more like conventional baking in colour, you do have to wait a short while for most ovens to preheat. However, it is not usually as long as for a conventional oven, because the cavity is smaller, and in combination halogen microwave ovens the preheat time is minimal as the heat is instantaneous.

Better Results

If you have not microbaked with wholemeal flour before, or are not used to recipes with less fat and sugar, the cakes and bakes may not seem as light or fluffy as those made with white products. However, many people are pleasantly surprised to find that microbaked wholemeal goodies *can* be far lighter than they thought possible. This is due in part to the fact that microbaked cakes, and microbaked wholemeal bread, form larger crumbs and have a more open texture, which counteracts any heaviness that might be supposed to accompany such items.

Some cooking methods are particularly successful with wholemeal ingredients, where they combine to enhance the lightness and wholesomeness. For example, sponges made by the whisked, Genoese or fatless methods are very easy and successful in the microwave. They also perform well when honey is used instead of sugar, and because honey adds moisture this counteracts any tendency towards dryness or quicker staling due to the higher after-baking temperatures.

Cakes and bakes made from batter mixtures (such as gingerbreads) are also especially well suited for microbaking because of their moistness. When microbaking you should make mixtures a little wetter than you would for baking in a conventional oven, but you will have to be careful about how much liquid you use in your recipes. Too much will result in heavy, unrisen bakes. Cakes with a high fruit content, too, are very suitable for the microwave because the fruit again adds moisture and flavour. Passion cake, carrot cake and banana cake are good examples.

What Does Microbaking Do to Your Food?

Wholemeal ingredients add more nutrients to your food and they also add fibre which is missing from refined flour. Eating more fibre is another healthy-eating goal for most adults (although the phytates found in wholemeal flour may bind with minerals – such as calcium, iron and zinc – and prevent them from being used by the body).

Scientists have looked at the effects of microbaking on fats and lipids in milk and egg yolks to see if they are chemically changed in the process, and therefore more likely to go 'off', and have come to the conclusion that there is no significant difference between microbaked and conventionally baked goods. Similarly there do not seem to be any unusual changes in the carbohydrates (starch, sugar and fibre) which are also major ingredients of baked foods.

However, there may be more to learn about these areas and about the effects on fibre in particular. Recent analyses of processed foods have shown that high temperatures cause retrogradation of starches (a normal process in cooking) to a greater degree than previously thought. The result is resistant starch (RS) which cannot be digested by the body's enzymes and so passes through the system like fibre. Whether RS has the health benefits of fibre, which is able to lower blood fats and improve digestive health, is still to be discovered, but it has a small benefit for slimmers in being, like fibre, a filler without the calories. Whether in fact microbaking, specifically, encourages the production of RS has yet to be established.

So far it seems that no research has been done into the effects of microwave baking on phytates, so we don't know if phytic acid is more or less problematic than in conventional baking. But experts at the Flour Milling and Baking Research Association think that in the context of a good mixed diet this is unlikely to give cause for concern – a standard, if not entirely satisfactory, response.

Reheating food causes more nutrients to be lost. Microbaked items likely to be reheated are pies, bread rolls, croissants. The lack of research into the effects of microbaking on nutrients in these foods is again because nutrition authorities think the amount consumed is unlikely to have a great effect on our nutritional status. Where fruits and vegetables are part of the recipe, the shorter cooking time in the microwave oven will mean that more nutrients are retained.

According to Institute of Food Technology tests, the flavour of microbaked goods improves on the second day after baking, which is true as well of some conventionally baked foods. The flavour of microbaked items has also been described as 'mild' or 'less flavoured' in these tests –

which of course is another reason why wholemeal and unrefined ingredients are ideal for obtaining better results.

Speedy Tips

There are several ways in which you can maximize the advantages of your microwave in order to ensure speed and success.

If you start with hot ingredients, such as melted fat and sugar in a flapjack or gingerbread recipe, then the baking time will be reduced.

The smaller, or thinner, the items are the quicker they will cook – but you do need to be careful with small items because timing is critical and any hot spots in your oven will produce burnt offerings. To test for hot spots you can place a series of ramekins full of water in the oven and heat on 'High' for a set time. If some boil over or heat before the others you will have identified hot spots and can avoid placing biscuits or similar small items in the same position.

Always mix well for even distribution of fat and sugar within the baked items to avoid hot spots caused by different foods cooking at different speeds. Fat and sugar, for example, cook more quickly than flour, and fresh fruit in baked goods cooks more quickly than dried fruit because it contains more water. Jams and syrups again cook quickly. Uniformly sized items, such as Chelsea buns and rock cakes, will also cook more evenly and there will be less likelihood that some will be overcooked while others are not ready.

Remember, as well, to turn the dish once or twice during the cooking, and to move its position in the oven even if the oven does have a turntable, to ensure even baking.

The more items you have in the oven, the longer will be the baking time. If one item takes about 20 seconds, two will take about 35 and three about 50. The denser the food is, too, the longer it will take to bake – a bread roll will bake more quickly than a potato. The type of ingredients will also affect the timing. For example, water has a heat specificity of 1.0 and fat of 0.5, so fat heats up twice as fast as water. In general, the higher the moisture content of the food, the more quickly it will be cooked.

A – Z of Microbake Ingredients

Agar-agar This is the vegetable equivalent of gelatine, and can be used by vegetarians as an alternative to this commonplace setting agent. Agar-agar is a naturally occurring derivative of seaweed. It is available from healthfood shops in powder form or as flakes. To use, sprinkle 2 level teaspoons on to a pint of cold water or other liquid before bringing to the boil, stirring occasionally to dissolve. (Two level teaspoons is the recommended amount, but for a less rubbery set use 1 teaspoon.)

If using gelatine, place the hot liquid in a container, sprinkle on 3 level teaspoons per pint of liquid and stir briskly until it is thoroughly mixed. Alternatively, sprinkle on to cold liquid and leave to soak before bringing to the boil, stirring all the time to dissolve. The gelatine/agar-agar will reach setting point once the liquid in which it has dissolved is cold. This process can be speeded by stirring the liquid while the container is standing on ice, or by refrigerating.

Almond butter A mixture of roasted crushed almonds and salt. Very similar to peanut butter, but sweet and tasty in biscuits.

Butter Unsalted butter is preferred for its flavour and lack of salt. (See also Margarine.)

Carob/chocolate Carob is a substitute for chocolate, available both in bars and in powder form. The advantages of carob are that it is naturally sweeter, so needing less sugar, and that it is free from additives, which some cocoa powders and drinking chocolates are not. It contains more calcium than chocolate, less oxalic acid – making it less likely to cause skin blemishes – and no tyramine or phenylethylamine, both of which can trigger migraines after eating chocolate. Above all it is free from caffeine and theobromine, both of which are stimulants and possibly addictive. Always sift carob powder because it tends to be lumpier than cocoa, and remember to store in a dry place. Carob bars will melt in the same way as chocolate and are easier to use for coating and dipping because you do not have to carefully 'temper' (gently heat and reheat) carob as you do chocolate. It can be melted and mixed with a little vegetable oil, vegetable fat, or skimmed milk powder to give it a glossier appearance.

Cheese   For long highly regarded as a source of protein, cheese is now used more moderately because of its high saturated fat content. In these recipes lower-fat soft cheeses are generally preferred. To cut down on fat in recipes using hard cheese, choose either a mature, strong-flavoured cheese – so a little will go a long way – or a lower-fat version of a traditional hard cheese such as Cheddar. There are supermarket own-brands and slimmers' brands of the latter which contain half the fat of normal hard cheeses.

Coffee   Wherever a recipe calls for coffee flavouring, decaffeinated coffee has been specified. This can be bought as instant soluble coffee, as ready-ground for use with filter machines and percolators, or as beans to grind for yourself.

Concentrated fruit juices   These can be used to soak dried fruit (see below) or to add a little moisture and sweetness to fruit cakes and other baked foods such as biscuits. Although dried fruit still contains sugar it is not so refined as sucrose (table sugar), and it also adds moisture which is a benefit for microbaking and counteracts a tendency towards dryness.

Dried fruit   Gives a recipe a natural sweetness without adding refined sugar. Soaking fruit overnight in fruit juice will enhance the sweetness and plump the fruit. If you want to avoid dried fruit that has been treated with preservatives and coated with mineral oils, read the labels and look for sun-dried fruits and fruits that are free from oils or are coated with vegetable oil.

Eggs   Free-range eggs are now widely available and are used here because the chickens are not fed dyes in their food to colour the yolks. Battery hens are fed such dyes as their unhealthy living conditions produce pale yolks. Free-range chickens are also less likely to be fed antibiotics and other drugs, and some studies have shown the eggs to contain more vitamins than battery eggs. Shoppers may also prefer free-range eggs for humanitarian reasons.

Size 3 eggs are used in all recipes unless otherwise stated.

Essences   Where flavourings such as almond or vanilla are required, natural essences are used. 'Flavourings' are avoided, as they are synthetically made. For orange, lemon and grapefruit flavours, natural oils are used.

Flour Wholemeal flour is specified because it contains all of the grain, to which nothing has been added and from which nothing has been removed. Wholemeal flour is rich in B vitamins and vitamin E, which are lost in the milling of white flour. It also contains minerals and fibre from the bran layer of the wheat.

Generally, it is enough to keep 100 per cent wholemeal in the storecupboard and add baking powder or bicarbonate of soda as required rather than using a self-raising flour which contains a predetermined amount of raising agent, although you can also buy self-raising wholemeal flour. In a few recipes strong, unbleached white flour is used to add variety. For choux pastry the best results, especially if you are not used to working with wholemeal flour, are often obtained with 85 per cent wholemeal – this has had part of the bran removed. (NB. Choux pastry is suitable only for combination microbaking.) Wholemeal flour is sieved to introduce air. Unless otherwise instructed, the bran in the sieve should be returned to the flour to be combined in the recipe. Discarding the bran would negate one of the main reasons for using wholemeal flour, namely to increase fibre intake.

Granary flour is used in some recipes and this is a registered trade name. It contains less fibre because it is a brown flour to which malted grains have been added (malted grains are moistened, germinated and then roasted.) Brown flour is not wholemeal – the extraction rate can be anywhere between 85 and 90 per cent. Malted flours may be coloured with caramel.

Rye flour is also used in some recipes. Again this is not usually wholemeal, but of a higher extraction rate.

Fructose This is the naturally occurring sugar in fruit, which is extracted to make a sugar that looks like the white variety but has slightly larger granules. It is used in smaller quantities because it is sweeter than sucrose (and because it is expensive!) It is less disruptive to blood sugar levels than sucrose, which is why it is often used in diabetic foods.

Gelatine See Agar-agar.

Honey This is a mixture of fructose and glucose, and as such it is really just another sugar to be used in moderation. Honey contains about 20 per cent water, which is useful because microbaking tends to produce drier results. It is especially successful for making whisked sponges as it whisks to a large volume with the eggs. Because of its pronounced flavour (as well as its sweetness) it also tends to encourage use of a little less sweetener, which is a good thing. However, where subtlety is required you can choose a light, clear honey which will have a more delicate flavour. Honey does contain vitamins and minerals, which sugar does not, but they are present in minute amounts which are nutritionally insignificant.

Jam Ordinary jam is high in sugar because it is the saturation by sugar that preserves the fruit. Yet some jams still contain preservatives, colourings and other additives. However, Extra Jam contains more fruit and no additives. No-added-sugar jams, of which there are now a wide range, can also be additive-free, but read the labels to check. They are set in pectin in the absence of sugar, and usually sweetened with grape juice. They are delicious and far more fruity than conventional jams. They make excellent glazes for microbaked items and can be used as purées because they are rich in fruit. They should be stored in the fridge once opened.

Margarine Most of the recipes in this book suggest soft vegetable margarine because it is likely to be high in polyunsaturates, as opposed to butter which has high levels of saturated fat. However, not all margarines are 'high in polyunsaturates' – they will carry this phrase if they are. Block margarines designed for cooking do not come into this category. They are made from vegetable oils or animal oils, but because they are hard they will have been hydrogenated and this saturates any unsaturated fatty acids. One hard fat that is high in polyunsaturates is White Flora.

Vegetable oils that are high in polyunsaturates (sunflower, safflower, corn and soya, for example) can be used in place of margarine for making pastries, if preferred. Low-fat spreads are not suitable for baking because they are emulsions which contain a lot of water. (This is why they are lower in calories than butter and margarine – which, incidentally, both contain virtually the same number of calories.)

Milk Whole milk (silver top) is high in saturated fat, so the recipes here use skimmed milk, which also has the advantage of containing 100 calories per pint compared with about 250 for whole cream milk.

Molasses This is made from the leftovers of the sugar cane once all the other products have been extracted. It is a dark syrupy liquid and should be stored in a cool, dry place because it is liable to ferment. Blackstrap molasses is the richest in nutrients. It adds colour and flavour to sweet bakes such as gingerbread. Being liquid, it is especially suitable for microbaking.

Salt On average we eat ½oz (12g) a day, which according to health experts is too much and should be cut by a quarter since salt is linked with obesity and heart disease. Shop-bought baked goods and processed foods add significant amounts of salt to our diet, but fresh and dried herbs and spices can be used in microbaked items as alternatives, or to help reduce the amount of salt eaten. Gradual reduction in other baked goods is advisable to wean the palate gently. Where salt is included in a recipe, sea salt is preferred because it contains more minerals and no additives.

Sugar Unrefined raw cane sugars are used for their superior colour, flavour and quality when compared to white refined sugars. Muscovado is a good general-purpose sugar for microbaking, available as both light and dark – light muscovado being suitable where a lighter colour and slightly more subtle flavour is required. Demerara is used for crunchy texture or for the crispness it imparts to flapjack-style recipes, and molasses (see above) where a rich dark colour and flavour is required in recipes such as gingerbread or for Christmas recipes. Look for genuine raw cane sugars and do not be fobbed off with poor quality white sugars and brown sugars such as 'London' demerara, which are just white sugars that are dyed brown with molasses extracts. Choose sugars refined from cane and marked with their country of origin.

Greek yoghurt   Thick and creamy Greek yoghurt is higher in fat than standard yoghurt (compare 10 per cent with 1 per cent), but much lower than double cream (48 per cent) which is conventionally used in mousse-type gâteau fillings and toppings. It has the same creamy consistency as whipped double cream, but without the calories (135-145 per 100 ml as against 447). Greek and Greek-style yoghurt has had all the whey (watery part) strained off, so it can hold its shape and texture in cakes and fillings for a short time, but to make it last longer bind it with a little setting agent such as gelatine. For a piping cream made with strained yoghurt, sprinkle ½oz (12g) gelatine on to 4 tablespoons cold water and microwave on High/600W for 60 seconds, remove and stir until dissolved. Leave to cool and when on the point of setting stir into 8oz (225g) strained yoghurt together with 2 drops natural vanilla essence. Whisk a free-range egg white until it is stiff and fold into the mixture. Chill for about 30 minutes before placing in a piping bag and using to decorate a trifle, as a filling for eclairs and profiteroles, or as a gâteau topping or filling.

For a chocolate cream, melt a small bar of plain chocolate or carob in the microwave and then stir into the yoghurt instead of the vanilla.

Glazes and Decorations

Glazes and decorations are especially important with microbaked goods for giving them an appetizing appearance. Although combination cooking will produce baked foods with instant eye-appeal, conventionally microbaked items – no matter how delicious they taste – will be duller in appearance and not have equal appeal unless they are garnished and decorated.

The absence of surface browning means that different glazes need to be used for microbaking. A clear honey or apricot glaze, for example, will be very suitable for giving appeal to microbaked wholemeal pastries. Traditional egg washes can also be used on microbaked items, and will give them a moist appearance, but they will not give a browned effect unless the items are placed under a grill where the surface will be exposed to radiant heat. Foods baked in a combination oven, on the other hand, can be glazed effectively with standard egg wash (or the equivalent) because surface browning is produced by the conventional heat.

Apricot glaze Take about half a jar of no-added-sugar jam (6-8 oz/175-225 g) and place in a dish with 2 teaspoons lemon juice and 2 tablespoons water. Cook on High/600W for 2 minutes, stir with a fork and cook for a further 2 minutes. Sieve if necessary, and place in a clean screwtop jar. When cold, cover with the lid and store in the fridge.

Alternatives: use any other jam of your choice for different flavours and different-coloured glazes.

Honey glaze Brush bread items such as Chelsea buns with clear honey while they are still hot for a sweet shiny glaze. Brush again, if liked, just before serving.

Egg wash Pastries cooked in a combination oven can benefit from being brushed with egg wash, as can microbaked items which are finished off under a grill to brown them. To make the egg wash, lightly beat one egg with 2 tablespoons milk. Unused egg wash can be stored in a covered container in the fridge for 2-3 days.

Alternatives: single cream or top of the milk will produce similar results.

Egg white Lightly beaten egg white is a good glaze for items such as biscuits. It gives a translucent effect when used in a combination oven. For microbaking it will give a moist appearance, and will help brown baked items if they are placed under the grill after baking.

Fruit glacé icing Although sugar is strictly speaking better left out of the diet, a little glacé icing on baked goods such as rich tea breads, or some yeasted buns, and cakes and sponges will enhance the finish and not add a great deal of sugar to a good mixed diet. To make fruit glacé icing, squeeze half an orange and strain the juice, a little at a time, on to 4 oz (100 g) sifted icing sugar, stirring well until it is thick enough to coat the back of a wooden spoon. This is particularly good for microbaked items which have not been finished with a glaze.

Alternatives: use other citrus fruit such as lemon, lime or grapefruit, or mix the sugar with orange, lemon or grapefruit essences or oils. You can also use any fruit juices or drinks for different colours and flavours.

Carob glacé icing Use the same amount of icing sugar, but sift in 1 tablespoon of carob powder (or cocoa powder if you prefer) and mix with 1½ tablespoons warm water as for fruit glacé icing.

Icing sugar Victoria sponges traditionally have a dusting of icing or caster sugar on the top. A variation on this theme is to dust the icing sugar through a sieve and over a doily placed on top of the sponge. Remove the doily to reveal a 'lace' topping to the cake – especially successful on carob cakes and darker wholemeal cakes.

Fruit juice gel or glaze This is made by setting fruit juice with gelatine. It gives a professional look to microbaked items and is the type of glaze used on strawberry, and other fruit tarts in patisserie shops. Take ¼-⅓ pint (150-200 ml) fruit juice such as orange juice or a tropical fruit mixture and either sprinkle on 3 teaspoons gelatine and bring to the boil on High/600W, stirring every minute until dissolved, or dissolve the gelatine in 4 tablespoons boiling water and stir into the fruit juice. Leave to cool and when on the point of setting – about 20 minutes – spoon over the gâteau or tart to be glazed. You can speed the setting by stirring the juice over ice, or refrigerating, but do not leave too long or the gel will set. (However, don't panic if it does because you need only warm it in the microwave and then wait for it to set again.)

Alternatives: use the juice from defrosted raspberries or cranberries to top fruit tarts or even to top meat-filled flans and pies. Red fruit juices such as redcurrant juice can also be used.

Low-fat frosting As an alternative to butter creams, why not try beating 8 oz (225 g) low-fat soft white cheese with ½-1 tablespoon clear honey and the juice and grated rind of half an orange or lemon. Use as a cake filling, or as a topping which can be smoothed with a palette knife or made rough and textured with a fork.

Carob frosting Melt a plain or flavoured carob bar with 2 tablespoons decaffeinated coffee on High/600W for 2-2.30 minutes. Mix with 4 oz (100 g) each of low-fat soft white cheese, and Greek yoghurt, then use as a frosting or a Swiss roll filling or fairy cake topping.

Sponge fillings/scone toppings No-added-sugar jams are delicious spread in sponges and Swiss rolls. Use them on their own, or spread a layer of jam then a layer of Greek yoghurt. Equally delicious as a combination for topping scones.

Crunchy topping Sprinkle a little Demerara sugar over the top of cakes before they are microbaked – especially successful with fruit cakes. You can also sprinkle Demerara sugar on to the greaseproof paper on which you turn out and roll up Swiss rolls.

Fruit and nut toppings Rather than thick royal icing on celebration cakes, top them with pretty arrangements of whole nuts – almonds, walnuts, pecans, hazlenuts – perhaps interspersed with whole glacé fruits or chopped pieces of dried fruits such as apricots and peaches. Stick these in place by brushing the top of the cake with apricot glaze, then brush the fruit and nuts with more apricot glaze when the arrangement is finished. (If using glacé cherries, choose the brands dyed with grape skins rather than artificial colourings.)

Alternative: roll out a thin layer of marzipan (no added colourings) and place on top of fruit cakes which have been brushed with apricot glaze. You can also use hand-rolled almond-shaped pieces of marzipan in the fruit and nut topping described above.

Microwaves and Microwave Equipment

How Microbaking Works

In conventional baking the heat is transferred from the hot air in the oven to the cakes, biscuits or bread being baked and the food is heated from the surface by convection. Other conventional methods of cooking include conduction – for example when samosas are dipped into hot fat – or radiation when the radiant energy from the toaster is carried through space to heat the surface of the bread to make toast.

By contrast, microwaves bake a cake without the need to heat the oven cavity and transfer the heat. Instead they enter the cake directly to agitate the water molecules, causing them to vibrate and create heat by friction inside the cake. The way it works is that every molecule is electrically positive, negative or neutral. When exposed to the electromagnetic microwaves the molecules jiggle around trying to line up with the waves, but as the waves keep 'moving' so do the molecules, and heat is created.

Contrary to popular belief microwaves do not cook foods from the inside out. They penetrate to just below the surface, losing their energy to the molecules in the food as they go. The heat generated by friction within the food is then taken by conduction to the centre of the item in the usual way. However, with smaller items such as biscuits the waves may cause the centre to heat up very quickly, so when you look at overcooked, spoiled biscuits it may seem as if they have cooked from the middle outwards. The short time taken to bake also means that timing is crucial; a few seconds too long may mean ruined biscuits. (A disadvantage of microbaking, however, is that the surface temperatures do not rise enough to actually brown the food.)

Microwave Safety

Microwaves are a non-ionizing form of radiation. This means that they are not like x-rays, nuclear radiation or other forms of radioactivity, and that they cannot cause damage to cells by interfering with cell division. So they will not cause 'mutations' in the food or in the people who eat it.

Microwave energy is a type of radiowave. The microwaves are contained within the oven cavity. If they leak you risk burns, but the energy dissipates quickly a short distance from the doors. Nevertheless, the British Standards Institute sets the maximum limit of leakage during the oven's life at 5 milliwatts (mW) per square centimetre (cm^2) at 5 cm from the door. Canada and some other countries have tougher standards of 1mW/cm^2 at 5 cm during the oven's life.

In commercial establishments safety checks to see that the oven is not leaking should be carried out twice a year, but for domestic ovens experts recommend an annual check. Leakage may occur around the door seals where damage can be caused if the oven is knocked or dropped, or the door twisted in some way. Domestic appliances are available for checking leakage, but a professional check is probably best. Environmental Health and Pollution Control (Findgraph Ltd), Camberley (0276) 684252 provide nationwide checks for which the current charge is £12 each. They do not repair ovens, so their results should be unaffected by any gain that might be made by recommending a repair.

Most burns in using microwave ovens result from scalds from hot liquids or from touching hot containers used to cook in the oven. Splashes and hot vapour (steam) can also cause injury in the same way as with conventional cooking. Exposure to the microwaves is rare, and if it happened you would feel pain, so damage could not occur without your realizing it. (However, you might not become aware of it until after the damage had been done, because the rays penetrate the skin very quickly to cause partial thickness burns before pain is registered.) Overall, as far as we know, microwave ovens remain safer than conventional ovens, not least because there are no boiling pans to be pulled or knocked from the hob. The sides of the oven remain cool and there are no exposed gas flames or electric elements.

There are a few rules from Findgraph to follow in order to make sure your oven stays safe:

- avoid operating without food inside
- do not scrub the door gasket with abrasives
- handle the door gently, and don't jam open while the oven is operating
- do not use if the door becomes loose
- stay away from the oven to reduce microwave exposure.

There have been some suggestions that exposure to radiowaves could cause subtle and cumulative effects on brain function, auditory function and nerves. However, these are very speculative and have not been corroborated. There are many other sources of similar radio frequency in the environment, for example from radio and tv, telecommunications and industry. Suggestions that microwave ovens might cause eye cataracts have not been proved, and some scientists say that under normal circumstances this could not occur.

Preparing for Success

If you already use a microwave oven you will be aware that unlike conventional ovens they are not all calibrated to the same temperature settings. 'High' may be 650W power in one microwave oven and 500W in another, and 'Medium' and 'Low' settings may differ similarly, so there is a greater element of getting to know your oven in microbaking than in conventional baking.

The recipes in this book have used 'High', 'Medium' and 'Low' settings as a general guide, but because of the wide variations of power and output in different ovens the terms are expressed as 'High/600W', 'Medium/360W' and 'Low/180W' to given an indication of the power levels used. However, there is still a need for some experimenting with your oven to make sure you interpret correctly the cooking temperatures and times.

Combination ovens use the same microwave settings in conjunction with standard, calibrated heat settings in centigrade or fahrenheit. The oven temperature is set in the usual way and the microwave power is turned on once the food has been placed in the oven.

Once you are familiar with your own oven and can judge the power output and performance, baking will be as easy as it is with conventional methods, but you will still have to use your judgment a little more because, just as fan-assisted ovens are faster than ovens without fans, so microwave ovens differ in speed of cooking. Even though recipes are designed to be followed exactly for best results, with the variations in power between microwave ovens there may be a need to adjust cooking times in your particular oven.

One big temptation is to put cakes back in the oven for an extra few minutes because they do not have the usual appearance of a conventionally cooked cake. They may appear to be a little moist on top, even when they are cooked, but you will soon get used to the fact that leaving them to stand for five minutes will finish the cooking and dry them out a bit. In some cases all that is required is to pat the top dry with absorbent kitchen paper.

Microbaked items are cooked when they have just begun to shrink from the sides of the dish – if they have shrunk in considerably then the cake will be overcooked and rubbery in consistency. During the cooling process they will dry out still more, and you will find that microbaked foods do

Microwaves and Microwave Equipment

stale more quickly than conventionally baked ones. This is because the post-oven temperature is higher than with conventional baking, which results in dehydration through evaporation.

You can also test microbaked items to see if they are cooked in the same way as conventional items by inserting a skewer or the point of a sharp knife. When this comes out clean the cake is cooked.

The best results will be obtained if you line the bases of baking dishes with greaseproof paper or baking parchment (also called silicone paper). If you don't, the bottoms of cakes may stick because they do not always dry out and come away from the base in the same way that conventionally cooked items do, even when they are ready. Only baked items that contain very little fat, such as breads, require the dish to be oiled.

You should also use deep dishes for sponges and cakes. Otherwise there is a danger that they will overflow, waste ingredients and make a mess in the oven, thus spoiling one of its main advantages – that of cleanliness. Never fill dishes more than two-thirds full.

Use round dishes, or dishes with rounded corners, which reduce the risk of overcooking in corner areas. Ring-shaped dishes (savarin moulds) are good for cakes, since they allow the microwaves to penetrate the food from the centre as well as the sides, top and bottom. A standard 7 inch (17.5 cm) cake dish is best. If the dish is too wide the cake will be soggy in the middle.

There is also a greater need to level the top of cakes and other mixtures before baking. The quicker cooking time will not permit the gradual levelling process that occurs in standard baking.

Microbake Cookware

There are many types of microwave cookware, from the flimsiest of simple throwaway plastic cake dishes to attractively designed durable heavy-duty ware that can also be used in combination ovens and conventional ovens up to a temperature of 220°C/425°F.

There are also probably many pieces of everyday cookware already in your kitchen that can be used for baking in the microwave oven – for example, glassware such as Pyrex, porcelain, china and other ceramic items. Even baskets and wooden containers can be used for reheating baked goods such as bread rolls and croissants. Not all of these, however, will be efficient for microbaking because they may not allow the microwaves to pass through to cook the food. The way to test cooking containers is to fill them two-thirds full with water and see if the microwaves boil the water quickly and efficiently without heating the container too much. You can test some of the flimsier microwave cookware in the same way to see if it becomes too hot to handle or unstable when lifted.

It is also important to know which utensils should *never* be used for microbaking. It might seem obvious, but it should be stated that metal bread tins, cake tins, bun trays, etc should not be used, as microwaves will not pass through metal (which is why the inside of the oven is metal, and why the glass door has a metal grid in it to deflect the microwaves back into the oven). If you try to bake in metal containers you will seriously damage your oven by reflecting the microwaves back on to the oven walls and on to the area from which they are emitted. Similarly, ceramic items with metal glazes and trims will risk damaging the oven and will interfere with even baking of the food by deflecting the microwaves away from it.

Although most microwave cookware is made from plastic of one sort or another, not all plastics are suitable, so check before use if you are in doubt. As a rule of thumb, if plastics are dishwasher proof then they should be suitable for use in the microwave. Certainly melamine or similar materials are not suitable because they absorb microwaves rather than letting them pass through to cook the food.

There are special cardboard containers for use in the microwave oven which look like paper party dishes. They are unsuitable for very high-fat dishes and are intended to be disposable, but they are useful for pies, flans, etc which are going to be frozen after cooking because they leave everyday dishes free for use.

Waxed paper cups and containers may appear to be suited to microbaking but they are not, because the wax will melt or migrate into the food if mixtures high in fat and sugar are baked in them. However, Cross Paperware carried out some tests for *The Wholemeal Microbake Book* baking sponge mixtures in their paper cups for hot drinks, which have a waterproof lining, and found that the cakes turned out well when cooked in batches of four for up to 2 minutes. They were not tainted and the lining was not affected. The manufacturers conclude that their cups for **hot drinks** are suitable for baking, but they stress that the results are from only one set of tests and that they cannot accept responsibility for any adverse affects. Neither have they tested other brands of paper cup.

Choosing Specialist Microbakeware

Caution is needed here, as even some microware is not in practice suitable for actual cooking. For example, 'freezer to microwave' trays and containers are designed for freezing conventionally cooked items once they have been cooled. They may be adequate for a short period of reheating, but not for cooking in. So read the packaging carefully and don't buy this type of container if you are looking for dishes to use for baking. Anchor Hocking's Chill Therm material, on the other hand, is used to produce all-in-one dishes which are suited to the freezer,

microwave and conventional oven through a range of temperatures from
0°F/−18°C to 400°F/200°C. Other manufacturers (see below) also
produce microware that can be used over this range of temperatures and
some, such as Adams' Micratex, is made from vitrified ceramic and is more
reminiscent of a dinner service than of microwave ovenware.

Because of the special requirements of microbaking, more than 30
companies produce specialist ovenware and accessories to match these
needs. Most are made from plastics. The British Plastics Federation, which
represents manufacturers, has a code of practice which covers materials
and how to mould them. It is also developing a test to determine an
allowable residual level of volatile components. In other words, it aims to
set a permissible level for 'migration' of plastics into the food.

Starter sets are made from the flimsier throwaway material that is not
designed to last and is more suitable for reheating than cooking. They are
supposed to be suitable for baking, although they are often labelled 'not
recommended for cooking high-fat or high-sugar foods'. Some baked items
might come into this category, but usually manufacturers are referring to
jam-making, syrups, bacon and sausages. It will probably be obvious from
their appearance, however, that these utensils should not be used when a
browning element is on, or with combination ovens, or in electric or gas
ovens, or on a hotplate or under a grill. They are often made from a flat
sheet of HDPE (high density polyethylene) which is stretched into shape
to make cake and pie dishes as well as utensils for other types of microwave
cooking. Cakes can be cooked in them up to a temperature of about
250°F/120°C but the dishes will discolour (although they can be reused),
and with high-fat or high-sugar recipes are unsuitable because they will
distort.

A slightly tougher material is PET (polyethylene terephthalate), which
is moulded and will take temperatures of up to about 400°F/200°C. It can
be used in combination ovens. It does stain slightly.

Rigid plastics are the most suitable for microbaking. These include
polycarbonate which can take temperatures of around 300°F/140°C, and
polysulfone which will take temperatures of 300-320°F/140-160°C.
Polyesters can be heavier and more rigid and take temperatures of 400-
410°F/200-210°C, as can a more popular material called TPX (methyl
pentene polymer) which is probably the most stain-resistant as well as
being non-stick. Although TPX is the most suitable, however, it is still
liable to distort in shape as it warms, or in the dishwasher. Large flat
surfaces are the most susceptible to distortion, with shapes such as savarins
and moulds being quite stable. Filling them with hot water and placing on
a flat surface should allow the material to come back into shape.

All microbake cookware has a high transparency to microwaves, being
between 97.5 and 99.8 per cent microwave transparent, compared with
glass which is 93-95 per cent microwave transparent – or less for some
types of glass. (However, microwave ware does sometimes become hot, so

it is still advisable to use oven gloves when removing items from the oven.)

As more and more microwave users are switching to combination ovens, it will probably save money in the long term to buy the more expensive and durable cookware, especially since it can also be used in conventional ovens at baking temperatures of up to about 425°F/220°C.

Specialist microbake ware is 'unbreakable' and does not chip or crack like ceramic and china or earthenware. It is shatterproof and non-stick. The materials it is made from are designed to resist stains, but if they do become stained then they should not be scrubbed with abrasive steel wool. The kind of scouring pad recommended for non-stick cookware is also suggested by microware manufacturers. Some recommend soaking in a solution of 50 per cent household bleach and 50 per cent water, after which the dish should be washed and dried and brushed with vegetable oil to restore colour and gloss. Others recommend proprietary brands of tea and coffee-stain removers.

Some manufacturers claim that research shows microbakeware should be designed with a rim to raise it off the base of the cooker (although shelves and turntables will also do this). This allows more even distribution of microwaves through the base to avoid cakes with soggy bottoms. The rounded corners also prevent food from being overcooked, and food is baked more efficiently in round containers rather than square or oblong ones. Often the sides are tapered for ease of food release.

Before using any microwave ware, give it a good wash in soapy water and then rinse and dry well. Remember that if you are using specialist microwave cookware your cakes will bake more quickly than if you are using glass or ceramic.

Bakeware Variety

There are now almost as many shapes and sizes of microwave cookware as there are of conventional. For example you can buy:
– fluted quiche dishes
– loaf pans
– sponge dishes
– sponge flan dishes
– deep cake (savarin) ring moulds
– individual ramekins for small cakes
– baking sheets (for buns and biscuits)
– bake ring (poaching set), also called muffin pan or ring
– browning skillet or tray (for griddled items).
A good basic microbake set should include a loaf dish, and a deep cake dish, with cake ring attachment or separate savarin base. If the oven

doesn't contain a tray on which to bake, then a baking sheet is also necessary.

Some dishes can be converted from a basic cake dish into a cake ring either by the insertion of a base with a central funnel, designed on the same lines as loose-bottomed cake tins, or by means of a simple funnel to place in the centre of the dish. You can improvise these dishes by placing a tumbler, coffee cup or ramekin in the centre of a cake or flan dish. The more useful cake dishes are loose-bottomed for easy removal and serving of standard cakes, flans and cheesecakes, but do not cut through with a metal knife because the cake dish base will be scored and damaged. Use a special microwave 'knife' made from plastic material.

If ramekins are used for individual cakes, the bases can be lined with paper to ensure the cakes do not stick and make it easier to remove them after cooking.

Some of the most sophisticated and easy-to-use baking dishes I have tried are made by WaveWare (my personal favourite), Micro Cuisine, Skyline (made by Prestige) and Thorpac. Good all-round dishes are also available from Lakeland Plastics' mail order catalogue.

Suppliers

William Adams Ltd, Furlong Road, Tunstall, Stoke-on-Trent ST6 5UB

Anchor Hocking Corporation, 271 High Street, Berkhamsted, Herts HP4 1AA

Corning Ltd, Wear Glass Works, Sunderland SR4 6EJ

Lakeland Plastics, Alexandra Buildings, Station Precinct, Windermere, Cumbria LA23 1BQ

Micro Cuisine, 77-79 Feeder Road, Bristol BS2 OTQ

Prestige Group plc, 14-18 Holborn, London EC1N 2LQ

Spong Housewares Ltd, Crumlin, Gwent NP1 4XF

Thorpac Group, Elliot Road, Love Lane Industrial Estate, Cirencester, Glos GL7 1LU

Clingfilm

The latest advice from the Ministry of Agriculture, Fisheries and Food is not to use clingfilm in microwave ovens unless the packaging states that it is suitable for microwave use, because harmful plasticizers can migrate into the food. Unlike other types of microwave cooking this is not a disadvantage in baking because cakes, breads, biscuits, etc are not covered during cooking as this would make them soft, soggy and unattractive.

Oven Cleaning

It is usually only necessary to wipe over the inside of the oven, but you should keep an eye on the door area to make sure that it does not collect dirt or debris as this could interfere with the seal. (Leakages are nevertheless said to be unlikely because of the double electronic safety mechanisms used in microwave ovens to ensure that they cannot be operated if the door is not properly closed.)

If the oven does become stained, some manufacturers recommend boiling a container of water in the oven to 'soak' off the food splashes. Strong abrasives should not be used inside the oven, but a little soapy water can be applied and rinsed off afterwards.

Combination Ovens

These allow the best of both worlds. Because they employ both convection and microwave heat, the speed of microwave cooking can be combined with the advantages of convection heat in browning the food.

While the results may be nearer to conventional baking, combination ovens do tend to cut down on the time saved because the food needs to be in the oven longer if browning is to take place. The best results are achieved if the food is cooked at higher 'conventional' temperatures and lower microwave powers, which makes the cooking time longer than with microwaves alone. For example, a sponge that would normally be baked at 350°F/180°C/Gas 4 can be baked at 375°F/190°C and a slightly lower power setting than for ordinary microbaking.

Combination cooking also means that you have to contend with the kind of baked-on stains and food splashes that occur in a conventional oven. However, they tend not to be as bad, probably because you do not put so much food in the oven at a time and because it is there for a shorter period.

Combination ovens may contain turntables or shelves and baking trays. Glass trays are usual for microwave and for combination cooking, although slatted metal trays may be used, but not solid metal trays which are suitable for convection cooking only, or for use with the oven's grill. You can bake two layers of items at once in some of the ovens, in which case the slatted shelf should be placed above the glass tray.

Some preheating may also be necessary, depending on the type of convection heat in the oven. Some have fan-assisted ovens which heat up quickly so that preheating is not necessary for all recipes, but it is usually needed for those which require very high temperatures. Combination ovens that use halogen heat are the most responsive because halogen heat filaments (which can be seen through windows in the roof and side of the oven) offer instant heat up to a maximum of 650W power, saving on time and money for any preheating. With halogen also there are no exposed heating elements as in other combination ovens, thus restoring some of the easy-clean attraction of the microwave.

Combination cooking is set to become the cooking method of the future because combination ovens offer the best of both worlds. They can brown and produce the traditional characteristics of baked and roast foods, whilst at the same time offering the enhanced speed of microwave power.

At one time they were available only to commercial establishments, but the industry has now recognized that the modern lifestyle, based on snack meals and fast foods, demands the same efficiency in a domestic situation. As microwaves become increasingly popular, with 25 per cent of homes owning a microwave oven – a figure estimated to reach 40 per cent by the 1990s – the switch to combination cooking looks inevitable. In America the four-microwave-oven household or family is by no means uncommon, because ovens are in use in the kitchen, living room, den and study, and on the patio for outdoor eating and use with the barbecue. This level of usage is not, however, expected to become typical in British households, where the microwave industry reports that we are more likely to exchange current models for new combination ovens.

And having learnt to 'cook' with a microwave, as opposed to using it solely for defrosting and reheating or melting, we are now looking for ways of extending our culinary expertise by exploiting the speed and cleanliness of the microwave oven in areas such as baking. Because combination cooking is so eminently suitable for microbaking, combination instructions are included throughout for the recipes in *The Wholemeal Microbake Book*, to provide for the cookery of tomorrow, as well as of today.

Microbake Checklist – Before You Start

– Remember to line bases of cake dishes and microwave baking trays with greaseproof paper, baking parchment or silicone baking paper.
– Unless otherwise stated, the bran in the sieve should be returned to the wholemeal flour to be combined in the recipe.
– Smooth the top of the mixture once it is in the dish.
– Make items such as biscuits and buns of even shape and size.
– Turn the dish once or twice during baking, or move its position even if the oven does have a turntable, to ensure even baking.
– Never cover cakes and breads or biscuits with a lid or film during cooking, because this will trap steam and prevent them from baking to a dry, or crisp, finish.

GRIDDLE BAKES

BROWNING SKILLETS can be used in the microwave oven as a griddle for making old-fashioned items such as drop scones. Such skillets are normally used for searing and browning (of course), but they make good griddles because they have even heat distribution and non-stick surfaces.

First the skillet is preheated in the microwave for the recommended length of time, then lightly greased with polyunsaturated margarine or oil to enhance the browning effect. The food is then placed on the skillet and cooked in the usual way.

Some browning skillets sit inside a tray which stays cool while the skillet reaches high temperatures. However, you should still place the hot skillet on a mat or trivet when transferring it to kitchen surfaces, and use oven gloves to remove it from the oven.

Between cooking batches of cakes or scones, paper towels are useful for wiping off any spills. Sometimes also the griddle loses heat between batches, in which case it should be reheated and oiled if necessary.

After cooking use hot soapy water – not abrasives or scourers – if there is a build-up of particles.

Oatcake

Serves 4-6
4 oz (100 g) fine or medium oatmeal
1 oz (25 g) soft vegetable margarine
½ tsp bicarbonate of soda
3 tbsp water

1. Preheat the griddle on High/600W for 6 minutes.
2. Place the oatmeal in a basin.
3. Put the margarine, bicarbonate and water in another basin and microwave on High/600W for 30 seconds to melt.
4. Mix the margarine and water, then pour into the centre of the oatmeal and mix with a fork to a soft and slightly wet consistency. Add a little more hot water if necessary.
5. Mould into a round and place on the preheated griddle which has been lightly oiled with a little margarine. Flatten slightly and return to the oven on High/600W for 2 minutes.
6. Remove and score into slices. Allow to become completely cold before cutting and eating.
7. Serve with cheese, or use in place of crispbread or crackers.

Honey Drop Scones and Welsh Cakes (page 4)

Sesame Cakes

Makes about 16
4 oz (100 g) wholemeal flour
½ level tsp baking powder
pinch sea salt
1 oz (25 g) light muscovado sugar
¾ oz (18 g) sesame seeds
1 free-range egg
⅛ pint (75 ml) skimmed milk
1 oz (25 g) soft vegetable margarine

1. Preheat the griddle on High/600W for 6 minutes.
2. Sift the flour, baking powder and salt into a mixing bowl. Stir in the sugar.
3. Sprinkle the sesame seeds on the preheated griddle and return to the oven on High/600W for 1.30 minutes to brown. Remove from the griddle and place on one side. Return the griddle to the oven and reheat for 2 minutes.
4. Lightly beat the egg and milk and pour into the centre of the flour. Gradually mix in with a fork.
5. Place the margarine in a basin and heat on High/600W for 30 seconds to melt.
6. Add the margarine to the mixture and stir in the sesame seeds.
7. Lightly grease the griddle with a little margarine and place 6 teaspoonfuls of the mixture around it. Bake on High/600W for 1.30 minutes. Turn over and bake for a further 30 seconds. Cool before eating.
8. Reheat the griddle for a couple of minutes before re-oiling to bake the next batch.

Marbled Carob Cookies

Makes about 16
4 oz (100 g) wholemeal flour
½ tsp baking powder
1 oz (25 g) dark muscovado sugar (optional)
1 oz (25 g) soft vegetable margarine
2 oz (50 g) malt extract
1 free-range egg
2 oz (50 g) carob chips, softened

1. Preheat the griddle on High/600W for 6 minutes.
2. Sift the flour and baking powder into a mixing bowl. Stir in the sugar, if using.

Cheese Baps (page 12), Granary Bread (page 11) and Wholemeal Soda Bread (page 9)

3. Place the margarine and malt extract in a bowl and melt on High/600W for 30 seconds.
4. Lightly beat the egg with a fork.
5. Add the egg to the flour and work in with a fork, then whisk in the melted margarine and malt extract. Finally fold in the carob chips – these will melt into the dough to create a marbled effect.
6. Lightly oil the griddle with some margarine and place 5 or 6 teaspoonfuls of the mixture, evenly spaced, on the griddle. Bake on High/600W for 1.20 minutes. Turn and cook the other side for 30 seconds.
7. Leave to cool and crisp on a cooling tray. Bake remaining cookies.

Note   The sugar is optional because malt extract is a natural sweetener and the biscuits are sweet enough for some tastes without the added sugar.

Welsh Cakes

Makes 6
4 oz (100 g) wholemeal flour
½ tsp baking powder
pinch sea salt
1 oz (25 g) soft vegetable margarine
1 oz (25 g) light muscovado sugar
2 oz (50 g) currants
1 free-range egg
2 tbsp milk

1. Preheat the griddle on High/600W for 6 minutes.
2. Sift the flour, baking powder and salt into a mixing bowl.
3. Rub in the fat until the mixtures resembles breadcrumbs in consistency.
4. Stir in the sugar and the currants.
5. Lightly beat the egg and make a well in the flour. Gradually add the egg, working it in with a fork.
6. Mix to a soft dough with the milk and then lightly roll out. Cut out 6 cakes using a 3 inch (7.5cm) pastry cutter.
7. Place the cakes on the lightly greased and preheated griddle and cook for 2 minutes, then turn over to cook for 30 seconds on the reverse side.

Honey Drop Scones

Makes about 15
4 oz (100 g) wholemeal flour
1 tsp baking powder

pinch sea salt
1 free-range egg
¼ pint (150ml) skimmed milk
1 large tbs clear honey

1. Preheat the griddle on High/600W for 6 minutes.
2. Sift the flour, baking powder and salt into a mixing bowl.
3. Lightly beat the egg and add to the skimmed milk.
4. Make a well in the centre of the flour and gradually work in the milk and egg using a fork.
5. Stir in the honey and whisk in well with the fork.
6. Lightly oil the griddle with some margarine and place 3 generous tablespoonfuls of mixture on the griddle.
7. Bake on High/600W for 60 seconds then turn over and bake for 30 seconds on the reverse.
8. Serve warm straight from the oven. Top with Greek-style yoghurt or sour cream and fresh or stewed fruit.

Waffles

Makes 6
4 oz (100 g) wholemeal flour
½ tsp baking powder
pinch sea salt
2 free-range eggs
⅛ pint (75ml) skimmed milk
2 oz (50 g) soft vegetable margarine

1. Preheat the griddle on High/600W for 6 minutes.
2. Sift the flour, baking powder and salt into a mixing bowl.
3. Lightly beat the eggs and make a well in the flour. Gradually whisk the eggs into the flour using a fork.
4. Gradually whisk in the milk.
5. Place the margarine in a basin and heat on High/600W for 30 seconds until melted. Pour into the flour and mix well.
6. Place 2 tablespoonfuls of mixture one on top of the other on the lightly oiled griddle. The mixture will spread out to make one waffle. Bake on High/600W for 1.30 minutes. Turn and cook for 40 seconds on the other side. Bake one waffle at a time.
7. Top with lemon juice and honey, or Greek-style yoghurt or fresh fruit or cottage cheese.

BREAD, CROISSANTS AND OTHER BREAKFAST BAKES

THE MAJORITY of these recipes use yeast – fresh baker's yeast which can be bought at baker's and at healthfood shops. As a general rule you will need to use ½ oz (12 g) fresh yeast to rise 1lb (450 g) flour and 1 oz (25 g) to rise up to 3lb (1.5 kg) flour or dough.

If fresh yeast is unavailable substitute dried yeast, bought most conveniently in sachets which usually contain around ¼ oz (7 g) and will do the same job as ½ oz (12 g) fresh yeast because with dried you need use only half the quantity. Dried yeast is also available in handy resealable tubs.

Both fresh and dried yeast are mixed with lukewarm water before being added to the flour. Fresh yeast is crumbled and stirred in, and used straight away. Dried yeast is stirred into about one-third of the liquid required in bread recipes and left to stand in a warm place until it froths. This is done to check that the yeast is still active and to start it working.

Although yeast needs heat to ferment the starches in the flour (this produces carbon dioxide which is trapped within the framework of the expanding loaf, making it rise), temperatures above 130°F/54°C will kill yeast.

Fast acting dried yeasts are also now available. They are combined with vitamin C and/or bread improvers (additives). These yeasts do not need reconstituting with water and can be stirred into the dry flour. Traditionally dough is kneaded for 5-10 minutes, left to prove and then knocked back and kneaded again before being put into a bread tin and left to double in size prior to baking. Fast-acting yeasts mean the dough is kneaded only once and put straight into the tin to double in size before baking, thus making considerable time savings. (You can, of course, apply this method with ordinary fresh and dried yeast, but the resulting loaf will be closer in texture and not so light as a double-kneaded and proved loaf.)

Yeasted recipes are much quicker in the microwave because proving and rising can be done in a fraction of the time. If you are already accustomed to using yeast, make the doughs a little wetter than normal because microwave baking can dry things out more easily. If you find that the ends of the loaves are dry, but the middles are softer, the cooking time is too long.

It is best to lightly oil loaf dishes because bread recipes do not contain much fat. Lining the base of the dish will also help towards successful breads. As with other bakes, do not cover the dishes while the items are cooking.

Soft Crumb Wholemeal Bread

Makes 1 large loaf
1lb (450 g) wholemeal flour
pinch sea salt
1 oz (25 g) soft vegetable margarine

½ pint (300 ml) water
½ oz (12 g) fresh yeast
1 dsp molasses

1. Sift the flour into a mixing bowl with the salt. Rub in the fat.
2. Warm the water in a jug on High/600W for 30 seconds. Remove from the oven, crumble in the yeast and mix to a paste.
3. Stir in the molasses and add the liquid to the flour. Mix to a soft dough and knead lightly for a minute or two on a lightly floured surface until elastic in consistency.
4. Return to the mixing bowl and prove on High/600W for 15 seconds. Remove from the oven, cover the bowl with a clean teatowel and leave to rest for 10 minutes.
5. Line the base of a 2½ pint (1.25 litre) loaf dish or terrine and lightly oil.
6. Knead the dough again and then shape and place in prepared dish. Repeat proving and resting twice. When the loaf has risen at least two-thirds of the way up the sides of the dish, bake on High/600W for 4 minutes.

Combination cooking Bake at 400°F/200°C on Medium/360W for 4.30 minutes. Finish off on conventional heat only for a further 3 minutes.

Wholemeal Soda Bread

Makes 1 large loaf
9 oz (250 g) 85 per cent wholemeal flour
1 tsp baking powder
1 tsp bicarbonate of soda
pinch sea salt
small tub natural yoghurt
⅓ pint (200 ml) skimmed milk

1. Sift the baking powder, bicarbonate and flour into a mixing bowl and stir in the salt.
2. Stir in the yoghurt and milk to make a soft dough and knead lightly on a floured surface.
3. Mould into an almond-shaped loaf and mark three slashes across the top using a sharp knife.
4. Bake on High/600W for 5 minutes. Stand for 5 minutes before attempting to cut. Serve same day.

Combination cooking Bake at 350°F/180°C on High/600W for 5 minutes.

Yeastless Brown Bread

Makes 1 large loaf
8 oz (225 g) wholemeal flour
8 oz (225 g) unbleached white flour
2 tsp baking powder
1 tbsp bran
pinch sea salt
12 fl. oz (360 ml) skimmed milk
rolled oats and cracked wheat to decorate

1. Line the base of a 1¼ pint (0.75 litre) loaf dish or terrine and lightly oil.
2. Sift the flours and baking powder into a mixing bowl and stir in the bran and salt.
3. Stir in the milk to make a soft dough. Knead very lightly on a floured surface and place in the prepared dish.
4. Brush with extra milk and lightly press in the oats and cracked wheat.
5. Bake on High/600W for 7 minutes.

Combination cooking Bake at 400°F/200°C on High/600W for 6 minutes, followed by 2 minutes on coventional heat only.

Rye Sourdough

Rye bread is traditionally very dense and microwave baking will not make it any lighter, but if you like rye bread and have the time to make a starter give this one a try and see if you prefer it to your usual rye bread recipe.

Makes 1 large loaf
½ quantity Sourdough Starter (see below)
¼ pint (150 ml) skimmed milk
4 oz (100 g) rye flour
6 oz (175 g) wholemeal flour
2 tsp baking powder
pinch sea salt
1 tbsp vegetable oil

1. Twenty-four hours before making the bread, take the sourdough starter and add the milk and rye flour. Mix well and leave to stand at room temperature.
2. Next day line the base of a 2½ pint (1.25 litre) loaf dish or terrine and lightly oil.
3. Sift the wholemeal flour with the baking powder and salt and stir into the rye mixture together with the vegetable oil.
4. Knead the dough on a lightly floured surface and place in the prepared

dish (alternatively, the dough can simply be made into a loaf shape). Prove in the oven on High/600W for 15 seconds. Cover while resting for 10 minutes and repeat twice.

5. Bake on Medium/360W for 7-8 minutes and remove from oven. Stand for 5 minutes in the dish before turning out to cool. Pat base dry if necessary.

Combination cooking Bake at 400°F/200°C on Medium/360W for 6 minutes. Finish off with a further 3 minutes on conventional heat only.

Sourdough Starter

½ pint (300 ml) lukewarm water (about 98°F/40°C)
1 sachet Allinson's Easybake yeast, or 1 sachet dried yeast and 1 × 25mg
  vitamin C tablet ground to a powder
4 oz (100 g) rye flour

Place the water in a large clean screwtop jar and stir in the yeast (and vitamin C, if necessary). Add the flour to make a smooth batter. Put the lid on and leave to stand at room temperature for 2 days.

Granary Bread

Makes 2 small loaves
1lb (450 g) Granary flour
pinch sea salt
2 oz (50 g) soft vegetable margarine
½ pint (300 ml) water
½ oz (12 g) fresh yeast

1. Sift the flour and salt into a mixing bowl, adding the grains from the sieve to the flour. Rub in the fat.
2. Place the water in a jug and heat on High/600W for 30 seconds. Remove from the heat and crumble the yeast.
3. Add the liquid to the flour and knead for 3 minutes until the dough is elastic, then return to the bowl and prove on High/600W for 15 seconds. Cover and leave to rest for 10 minutes.
4. Remove dough from the bowl and knead again. Form into two cottage-loaf shapes or place the dough in two 1¼ pint (0.75 litre) loaf dishes or terrines with bases lined and prove again, as before. Repeat once or until the dough has risen at least two-thirds of the way up the sides of the dishes or until it has doubled its size.
5. Bake on High/600W for about 8 minutes if baking the two loaves together, or for about 6 minutes if baking separately.

Combination cooking Bake at 400°F/200°C on Medium/360W for 6 minutes. Finish off with a further 3 minutes on conventional heat only.

Cheese Baps

Makes 10-12
1lb (450 g) wholemeal flour
pinch sea salt
½ pint (300 ml) water
½ oz (12 g) fresh yeast
4 oz (100 g) grated mature Cheddar or Double Gloucester

1. Sift the flour into a mixing bowl with the salt.
2. Heat the water in a jug on High/600W for 30 seconds. Remove from the oven and crumble in the yeast.
3. Pour the yeast mixture into the flour and mix to a dough.
4. Knead on a lightly floured surface for 3 minutes and then return to the bowl and prove on High/600W for 10 seconds. Leave to rest for 10 minutes.
5. Knead the dough again and roll out lightly so it is about 1½ inches (4 cm) thick and, using a plain-edge scone cutter, cut out 3 inch (7.5 cm) rounds.
6. Place on a lightly oiled or lined microwave tray and prove as before. Repeat once.
7. Sprinkle the grated cheese evenly over the top of the rolls and bake on High/600W for 3.30 minutes.

Combination cooking Bake at 400°F/200°C on High/600W for 3 minutes.

Note You can also make a Cheese Loaf by kneading the cheese into the dough before placing it in a prepared loaf dish. Prove and rise as for the rolls and bake on High/600W for 8 minutes or in a combination oven for 6 minutes, finishing off on conventional heat only for 3 minutes.

Traditional Croissants

Makes 12
12 oz (325 g) wholemeal flour
2 oz (50 g) unsalted butter
pinch sea salt
8 fl. oz (240 ml) skimmed milk
1 oz (25 g) fresh yeast
6 oz (175 g) unsalted butter from the fridge
apricot or honey glaze, or egg wash

1. Sift the flour and salt into a mixing bowl and rub in the 2 oz (50 g) of fat.

2. Place the milk in a measuring jug and heat on High/600W for
30 seconds. Remove from the heat and crumble in the yeast. Mix to a soft
dough with the flour and fat and knead lightly for 2 minutes. Cover and
rest for 10 minutes.
3. Flatten the 6 oz (175 g) of cold butter using a rolling pin on a floured
board.
4. Roll out the dough on a floured surface into a large rectangle 14 × 10
inches (40 × 25 cm). Place the butter over the bottom two-thirds of the
surface. Fold the unspread third down over the central third, then fold the
other third on top. Turn the dough sideways so the folded edges are left
and right. Roll again, away from you, to make a rectangle and repeat the
folding.
5. Cover and rest in the freezer for 10 minutes. Repeat the two double
folds and rest again. Wrap and return to the freezer for 15 minutes.
6. Repeat rolling and folding, and return to the freezer for a further 10
minutes or until you need the dough.
7. Roll out to a rectangle about 18 × 12 inches (45 × 30 cm) and cut out
the croissants. To do this first cut the dough in half down the length then
cut diagonally from the outer edges to the centre to make triangles. Roll
the triangles from the widest edge to the point to make the familiar
croissant shape, which can be left straight or bent into a crescent.
8. Place on a lightly oiled or lined microwave tray and prove on
High/600W for 15 seconds. Leave to rest for 10 minutes. Repeat twice
until doubled in size, then bake on High/600W for 5 minutes.
9. Remove from the oven and cool on a wire cooling tray. Glaze while
hot with clear honey or apricot glaze. Serve warm.

Combination cooking Bake at 400°F/200°C on Medium/360W for
4 minutes, then follow with a further 2 minutes on conventional heat
only. Glaze with egg wash.

Bran Croissants

Makes 8
10 oz (275 g) wholemeal flour
2 oz (50 g) bran
½ oz (12 g) fresh yeast
1 oz (25 g) soft vegetable margarine
ice-cold water
4 oz (100 g) soft vegetable margarine

1. Lightly oil or line a microwave tray.
2. Sift the flour into a mixing bowl and stir in the bran. Sprinkle on the
crumbled yeast. Rub in the 1 oz (25 g) of fat until the mixture resembles
breadcrumbs in consistency.

3. Mix to a soft dough with the iced water and knead on a floured surface for 3 minutes.

4. Roll out on a floured surface into a large rectangle about 14 × 10 inches (40 × 25 cm). Spread the 4 oz (100 g) of margarine over the bottom two-thirds of the surface. Fold the unspread third down over the central third then fold the other third on top. Turn the dough sideways so the folded edges are left and right. Roll again, away from you, to make a rectangle and repeat the folding.

5. Cover and rest in the freezer for 10 minutes, then repeat the two double folds and rest again. Wrap and return to the freezer for 15 minutes.

6. Remove from the freezer and roll into a circle on a lightly floured board. Cut into 8 segments. Roll each from the outside to the centre and then roll the croissants into their characteristic crescent.

7. Place on the prepared turntable or shelf and prove by placing in the oven on High/600W for 15 seconds. Cover and leave to stand for 30 minutes.

8. When risen bake on High/600W for 7 minutes.

Combination cooking Bake at 400°F/200°C on Medium/360W for 13 minutes.

Paper-Cup Brioches

For important further details about microbaking in paperware see page xxv.

Makes 6
8 oz (225 g) wholemeal flour
pinch sea salt
1 oz (25 g) fructose
4 tbsp water
½ oz (12 g) fresh yeast
2 oz (50 g) soft vegetable margarine
2 free-range eggs

1. Sift the flour into a mixing bowl with the salt. Stir in the fructose.

2. Measure the water into a small basin or ramekin and heat on High/600W for 30 seconds. Remove from the oven and crumble the yeast into the water.

3. Place the margarine in a small basin and heat on High/600W for 1.30 minutes to melt. Lightly beat the eggs.

4. Add the yeasted water and the eggs to the flour then stir in the melted margarine.

5. Knead the dough lightly and divide into six. Place a piece in each cup and then prove on High/600W for 15 seconds. Leave in the oven to rest for 10 minutes and then repeat twice. At the end of the third resting time the dough should have risen to the edge of the cups.

6. Bake on High/600W for 4 minutes. Carefully remove the cups from the oven and slip a knife between each brioche and the cup to loosen, then remove and allow to cool on a wire cooling tray.

Combination cooking Bake at 375°F/190°C on Medium/360W for 4 minutes followed by a further 1.30 minutes on conventional heat only.

Bran and Raisin Muffins

Makes 8
6 oz (175 g) wholemeal flour
1 tsp baking powder
2 oz (50 g) bran
3 oz (75 g) raisins
⅛ pint (75ml) skimmed milk
2 oz (50 g) soft vegetable margarine
1 tbsp molasses
2 oz (50 g) malt extract or barley malt syrup

1. Have ready a microwave bun tray with 8 cups.
2. Sift the flour into a mixing bowl with the baking powder and stir in the bran and the raisins.
3. Place the remaining ingredients in a jug or basin and heat on High/600W for 1.30 minutes. Remove and stir until dissolved.
4. Mix into the dry ingredients, divide the mixture between the bun cups and cook on High/600W for 4 minutes. These are nice served warm.

Combination cooking Bake at 375°F/190°C on High/600W for 3 minutes.

Banana and Nut Bagels

Makes 6
8 oz (225 g) wholemeal flour
tiny pinch turmeric
1 oz (25 g) unsalted butter
¼ pint (150 ml) water
½ oz (12 g) fresh yeast
1 small ripe banana
2 oz (50 g) chopped nuts of choice
apricot or honey glaze, or egg wash

1. Lightly oil or line a microwave tray.
2. Sift the flour into a bowl together with the turmeric. Rub in the fat until the mixture resembles breadcrumbs in consistency.

3. Heat the water in a jug or basin on High/600W for 30 seconds. Crumble in the yeast and mix to a paste.

4. Add the liquid, mashed banana and nuts to the flour and beat to a smooth dough.

5. Prove in the oven on High/600W for 15 seconds, cover and rest for 10 minutes.

6. Knock back on a lightly floured surface and divide the dough into six. Knead each piece lightly into a doughnut shape. Prove as before, but this time twice, by which time the bagels will have doubled in size.

7. Bake on High/600W for 4.30 minutes. Remove from the oven and glaze with honey or apricot or, if liked, paint with egg wash then brown carefully under the grill.

Combination cooking Bake at 425°F/218°C on High/600W for 3.30 minutes. Leave the bagels in the oven on conventional heat only for a further 3-4 minutes to brown and crisp.

Pretzels

Makes 8
8 oz (225 g) wholemeal flour
1 oz (25 g) soft vegetable margarine
¼ pint (150 ml) skimmed milk
½ oz (12 g) fresh yeast
egg wash and caraway seeds to decorate

1. Lightly oil or line a microwave tray.

2. Sift the flour into a mixing bowl. Rub in the fat until the mixture resembles breadcrumbs in consistency.

3. Heat the milk in a jug or basin on High/600W for 30 seconds. Crumble the yeast into the lukewarm milk and mix to a paste.

4. Mix the milk with the flour to make a soft dough. Prove in the oven on High/600W for 15 seconds, cover and rest for 10 minutes. Repeat.

5. Knock back the dough and make pretzel shapes. Divide the dough into 8 and roll very thinly into pieces about 18 inches (45 cm) long. Make a large horseshoe shape then twist the ends back on themselves and stick them to the sides to give the characteristic appearance.

6. Place on the prepared tray and prove once, as before. Brush with the egg wash and sprinkle over the seeds, then cook in two batches on High/600W for 4.30 minutes each.

7. Remove from the oven, reglaze and brown under the grill, if liked.

Combination cooking Bake at 425°F/218°C on High/600W for 3.30 minutes.

TEABREADS, BUNS AND SWEET PASTRIES

For notes on using yeast see introduction to preceding section, *Breads, Croissants and Other Breakfast Bakes*.

Marzipan Tea Ring

Serves 6
8 oz (225 g) wholemeal flour
2 oz (50 g) soft vegetable margarine
⅛ pint (75ml) skimmed milk
½ oz (12 g) fresh yeast
1 free-range egg (size 2)
4 oz (100 g) white or raw cane sugar marzipan
fructose to decorate

1. Sift the flour into a mixing bowl.
2. Rub in the fat until the mixture resembles breadcrumbs in consistency.
3. Measure the milk into a small basin or ramekin and heat on High/600W for 20 seconds. Remove from the heat and crumble in the yeast.
4. Lightly beat the egg and add the milk and egg (reserving a minute amount for glazing) to the flour. Blend to a soft dough and knead on a lightly floured surface for 2 minutes.
5. Return to the mixing bowl and prove on High/600W for 15 seconds. Rest for 10 minutes and then lightly knead and roll out into a rectangle about 14 × 4 inches (35 × 10 cm).
6. Soften the marzipan by putting in the microwave, unwrapped, on Medium/360W for about 30 seconds, then roll out into a long sausage.
7. Baste the edges of the dough and place the marzipan in the middle then fold over and seal the edges.
8. Bend the roll around to make a circle, placing the fold edge beneath the ring, and smooth together the join. Make little snips at regular intervals around the outer edge of the ring.
9. Prove twice, as before, then glaze with egg white, sprinkle with fructose and bake on High/600W for 4.30 minutes.

Combination cooking Bake at 400°F/200°C on Medium/360W for 4 minutes, followed by a further 2 minutes on conventional heat only.

Bath Buns

Makes 10
10 oz (275 g) wholemeal flour
½ oz (12 g) fresh yeast
1 oz (25 g) light muscovado sugar

Tutti Frutti Bun Wheel (page 22), Banana and Nut Bagels (page 15) and Bath Buns (page 18)

3 oz (75 g) sultanas
1 oz (25 g) mixed peel
¼ pint (150 ml) skimmed milk
1 oz (25 g) soft vegetable margarine
1 free-range egg (size 2)
fructose to decorate the tops of the buns

1. Sift the flour into a mixing bowl. Crumble in the yeast.
2. Stir in the sugar, sultanas and peel.
3. Place the milk and margarine in a jug, heat on High/600W for 1.30 minutes and add to the dry ingredients.
4. Lightly beat the egg and add to the mixture.
5. Place on a lightly floured surface and knead for 2 minutes. Place 10 tablespoonfuls of dough on a lightly oiled microwave tray and prove for 15 seconds on High/600W. Leave to rest for 10 minutes.
6. Repeat twice and then sprinkle the tops with a little fructose and bake on High/600W for 3.30 minutes.

Combination cooking Bake at 400°F/200°C on Medium/360W for 3 minutes, followed by a further 1.30 minutes on conventional heat only.

Peach and Apricot Pastries

Makes 8-10
8 oz (225 g) wholemeal flour
pinch sea salt
1 oz (25 g) soft vegetable margarine
¼ pint (150 ml) skimmed milk
½ oz (12 g) fresh yeast
1 oz (25 g) light muscovado sugar
2 oz (50 g) each dried peaches and apricots
¼ pint (150 ml) fruit juice
apricot glaze

1. Sift the flour into a mixing bowl with the salt. Rub in the fat.
2. Warm the milk in a jug on High/600W for 30 seconds. Remove from the heat and crumble in the yeast.
3. Stir the sugar into the flour and then pour on the yeast liquid and mix to a soft dough.
4. Knead lightly on a floured surface, then return to the bowl and prove on High/600W for 15 seconds. Remove from the oven, cover with a clean teatowel and leave to rise for 10 minutes.
5. Meanwhile, place the fruit in a dish with a lid together with the fruit juice, cover and cook on High/600W for 3-4 minutes until soft. Remove and purée by mashing with a fork or liquidizing.

Mincemeat and Apple Plait (page 23) and Tea Brack (page 24)

6. Roll out the dough on a lightly floured surface and cut into 2½ inch (7.5 cm) squares. Spread the purée mixture diagonally across each square, then fold over the other two diagonally opposite corners to partially envelope the filling.

7. Place on the lightly oiled or lined microwave shelf and glaze with a little apricot glaze, then prove on High/600W for 15 seconds. Leave in the oven to rest for 10-15 minutes until well risen, then bake on High/600W for 3.30 minutes.

Combination cooking Bake at 400°F/200°C on Medium/360W for 3 minutes. Finish off on conventional heat only for a further 2 minutes.

Malted Teabread

Serves 8
8 oz (225 g) wholemeal flour
1 tsp mixed spice
2 oz (50 g) soft vegetable margarine
6 oz (175 g) mixed dried fruit
⅛ pint (75 ml) skimmed milk
2 tbsp malt extract
½ oz (12 g) fresh yeast
1 free-range egg
apricot or honey glaze, or egg wash

1. Lightly oil a 2½ pint (1.25 litre) loaf dish or terrine and line the base.

2. Sift the flour and spice into a mixing bowl. Rub in the fat until the mixture resembles breadcrumbs in consistency.

3. Stir in the dried fruit.

4. Place the milk and malt extract in a jug or basin and heat on High/600W for 60 seconds. Crumble the yeast into the milk and mix to a paste.

5. Lightly beat the egg, add the egg and milk to the flour and mix to a dough.

6. Place on a lightly floured surface and knead for 2 minutes. Roll into a thick sausage about twice the length of the terrine, fold under both ends to meet in the middle and place, folded side down, in the prepared dish.

7. Prove on High/600W for 15 seconds. Cover and stand for 10 minutes. Repeat twice.

8. Bake on High/600W for 6 minutes. Remove from oven and, if liked, glaze the top with egg wash and brown carefully under the grill.
Alternatively glaze while hot with jam or honey.

Combination cooking Glaze with egg wash and bake at 400°F/200°C on High/600W for 4 minutes.

Pineapple Pastries

Makes 12
8 oz (225 g) wholemeal flour
pinch sea salt (optional)
1 oz (25 g) soft vegetable margarine
1 dsp fructose
½ oz (12 g) fresh yeast
⅛ pint (75 ml) lukewarm water
1 free-range egg
4 oz (100 g) unsalted butter, cold
1 small can pineapple rings
fruit glacé icing

1. Lightly oil or line a microwave tray.
2. Sift the flour and salt into a mixing bowl. Rub in the fat until the mixture resembles breadcrumbs in consistency.
3. Stir in the fructose.
4. Crumble the yeast into the water.
5. Lightly beat the egg, add the egg and the yeast mixture to the flour, and mix to a soft dough. Knead lightly for a couple of minutes then roll out the dough to a rectangle about 12 × 8 inches (30 × 20 cm).
6. Flatten the butter into a rectangle so that it covers about two-thirds of the dough. Fold the remaining third up over the butter and then fold the other buttered piece over that to envelope the butter. Turn once so the folded sides are to the left and right. Roll out and repeat the folding.
7. Cover the dough and place in the freezer for 10 minutes. Remove and repeat the rolling and folding twice more.
8. Roll out thinly to a large rectangle and cut into 12 squares of about 4 × 4 inches (10 × 10 cm). Place half a pineapple ring in each and fold up the corners to envelope the pineapple in pastry.
9. Carefully lift on to the tray and prove on High/600W for 15 seconds. Leave in the oven to rest for 10 minutes. Repeat, then bake on High/600W for 5 minutes. Remove and cool on a wire tray.
10. Decorate with fruit glacé icing.

Combination cooking Bake at 375°F/190°C on Medium/360W for 6 minutes.

Mixed Fruit Twist

Serves 8
12 oz (325 g) wholemeal flour
4 oz (100 g) soft vegetable margarine
3 oz (75 g) mixed dried fruit and peel

¼ pint (150 ml) skimmed milk
½ oz (12 g) fresh yeast
1 free-range egg
2 tbsp plum jam, plus extra to glaze

1. Lightly oil or line a microwave tray.
2. Sift the flour into a mixing bowl. Rub in the fat until the mixture resembles breadcrumbs in consistency. Stir in the dried fruit.
3. Heat the milk in a jug or basin in the oven on High/600W for 60 seconds until it is lukewarm but not hot, then crumble in the yeast.
4. Lightly beat the egg, then add the egg and milk to the flour mixture.
5. Knead the dough on a floured surface for a minute and roll out to a 12 x 8 inch (30 x 20 cm) rectangle. Spread the jam over the dough and roll up as you would a Swiss roll.
6. Place on the tray and make incisions at about 1 inch (2.5 cm) intervals in the roll, but do not cut completely through. Alternately pull out one 'bun' to the left, the next to the right, to make an attractive twist. Prove in the oven on High/600W for 15 seconds. Cover and rest for 10 minutes. Repeat the proving twice more until the twist has doubled in size.
7. Bake on Medium/360W for 10 minutes followed by 2 minutes at High/600W. Glaze while still hot with more jam.

Combination cooking Bake at 400°F/200°C on High/600W for 4 minutes.

Tutti Frutti Bun Wheel

Serves 8
4 oz (100 g) mixed 'exotic' dried fruits (e.g. apple, pear, peach, prune)
10 oz (275 g) wholemeal flour
2 oz (50 g) soft vegetable margarine
¼ pint (150 ml) skimmed milk
½ oz (12 g) fresh yeast
1 dsp malt extract
extra malt extract or jam for glazing

1. Lightly oil or line a microwave tray.
2. Soak the dried fruit overnight or place in a dish with a lid, with enough water to almost cover, then cook on High/600W for 4 minutes. Stir and return to cook for another 2 minutes.
3. Sift the flour into a mixing bowl. Rub in the fat until the mixture resembles breadcrumbs in consistency.
4. Heat the milk in a jug or basin on High/600W for 20 seconds, remove from the oven and crumble in the yeast. Stir to make a paste and add the malt extract at the same time.

5. Pour the liquid on to the flour and mix to a soft dough. Place on a floured surface and knead for 3 minutes. Roll into a rectangle 12 × 8 inches (30 × 20 cm).
6. Spread the fruit over the dough and roll up as you would a Swiss roll. Cut the roll into 8 and place the buns, touching, with cut sides down, on the prepared shelf. Put 7 round the edge and one in the centre, in a wheel arrangement.
7. Prove on High/600W for 15 seconds, then leave to rest for 10 minutes. Repeat once or twice until doubled in size.
8. Bake on High/600W for 7-8 minutes. Glaze when hot with more malt extract or jam.

Combination cooking Glaze and bake at 400°F/200°C on High/600W for 10 minutes.

Mincemeat and Apple Plait

Serves 6-8
8 oz (225 g) wholemeal flour
½ pint (300 ml) lukewarm water
¼ oz (6 g) fresh yeast
2 large cooking apples
½ lemon, juice of
4 oz (100 g) mincemeat
jam to glaze

1. Lightly oil or line a microwave tray.
2. Sift the flour into a mixing bowl.
3. Crumble the yeast into the water, and stir into the flour to make a soft dough. Knead on a floured surface for 2 or 3 minutes. Place in a bowl in the microwave and prove on High/600W for 15 seconds. Leave to rest, covered, for 10 minutes.
4. Meanwhile peel and core the apples and slice. Toss at once in the lemon juice to prevent browning. Place in a dish with a lid, add 2 tbsp water, cover and cook on High/600W for 1.30 minutes to soften the apple.
5. Roll out the dough to a rectangle 12 × 8 inches (30 × 20 cm). Spread the mincemeat over the dough, leaving a 2 inch (5 cm) gap all round the edge. Arrange the apple slices neatly on the top in rows.
6. Cut the long sides of the dough from the filling to the edge at intervals of 1 inch (2.5 cm). Fold the cut pieces up over the filling, overlapping slightly, and then glaze with jam.
7. Bake on High/600W for 6 minutes.

Combination cooking Bake at 400°F/200°C on Medium/360W for 7 minutes. Finish on conventional heat only for 4 minutes.

Fruity Tea Ring

Serves 8-10
¼ pint (150 ml) skimmed milk
1 free-range egg yolk
2 tbsp skimmed milk
2 tbsp maple syrup
½ oz (12 g) fresh yeast
8 oz (225 g) wholemeal flour
3 oz (75 g) mixed fruit and peel
1 oz (25 g) walnuts, chopped finely
apricot spread or clear honey to glaze

1. Lightly oil a glass savarin mould.
2. Place the milk in a jug and warm on High/600W for 30 seconds. Beat the egg yolk with the 2 tbsp of milk and stir into the warmed milk, together with the syrup. Crumble in the yeast and mix to a paste.
3. Sift the flour into a mixing bowl and stir in the fruit and the nuts.
4. Add the liquid and lightly knead to a soft dough. Place in a bowl and prove in the microwave on High/600W for 20 seconds. Cover the bowl and leave to rest for 10 minutes. Repeat.
5. Lightly knock back the dough and roll into a sausage to fit the dish. Double prove as before, then bake on High/600W for 4 minutes.
6. Remove from the oven and turn out of the dish on to a cooling tray. Brush the top with either clear honey or apricot spread. Glaze again just before serving.

Combination cooking Bake at 400°F/200°C on High/600W for 10 minutes.

Tea Brack

Serves 8-10
4 oz (100 g) sultanas
4 oz (100 g) currants
1 tsp each ground cinnamon and mixed spice
1 oz (25 g) dark muscovado sugar
pot of cold tea
8 oz (225 g) wholemeal flour
1 tsp baking powder
2 free-range eggs

1. Soak the dried fruit, sugar and spices overnight in the cold tea. Don't forget to pour it through a strainer – you don't want to add the leaves to the mixture.

2. Next day sift the flour and baking powder into a bowl and lightly beat the eggs.

3. Line the base of a 2½ pint (1.25 litre) loaf dish or terrine and lightly oil.

4. Strain the fruit, reserving the liquid, and add the fruit to the flour at the same time as the beaten eggs. Blend well to make a soft consistency, adding a little of the cold tea.

5. Place in the loaf dish and smooth the top. Bake on Medium/360W for 6 minutes.

6. Remove from the oven and stand in the dish for 5 minutes. Turn out on to a cooling tray and peel the paper off the base.

Combination cooking Bake at 350°F/180°C for 5 minutes, followed by a further 4 minutes on conventional heat only.

Note This recipe is most successful if cooked in a combination microwave, although you can also cook it in a standard microwave oven.

Raisin Bread

Serves 10
10 oz (275 g) wholemeal flour
1 tsp cinnamon or Swedish kardemumma
6 oz (175 g) large seeded raisins
¼ pint (150 ml) skimmed milk
pinch saffron strands
2 oz (50 g) soft vegetable margarine
1 tbsp clear honey
½ oz (12 g) fresh yeast
clear honey or egg wash to glaze

1. Sift the flour into a mixing bowl together with the spice and stir in the raisins.

2. Place the milk in a jug with the saffron, margarine and honey and heat on High/600W for 1.30 minutes to melt.

3. Remove and stir well then crumble in the yeast. Stir again and pour on to the flour mixture and work to a soft dough with a fork. Prove on High/600W for 15 seconds and leave to stand for 10 minutes either in the oven or covered with a clean teatowel in a warm place. Repeat once.

4. Remove from the bowl and lightly knead for a minute then place in a lightly oiled fancy mould, loaf dish or soufflé dish and bake on High/600W for 7 minutes.

5. Remove and glaze while hot with honey, or glaze with egg wash and lightly brown under the grill.

6. When cool enough to handle remove from the dish and leave to dry and cool on a wire baking tray.

Combination cooking Bake at 400°F/200°C on Medium/360W for 8 minutes.

Chelsea Buns

Makes 9
8 oz (225 g) wholemeal flour
1 oz (25 g) vegetable margarine
½ oz (12 g) fresh yeast
¼ pint (150 ml) skimmed milk
1 oz (25 g) soft vegetable margarine or unsalted butter
1 oz (25 g) light muscovado sugar
2 oz (50 g) mixed dried fruit
2 oz (50 g) mixed peel

1. Sift the flour into a bowl and rub in 1 oz (25 g) of fat until it resembles breadcrumbs in consistency.
2. Place the milk in a jug and heat on High/600W for 30 seconds until it is lukewarm, then crumble in the yeast and stir well.
3. Pour the milk on to the flour and work to a dough. Knead on a floured surface for 5 minutes, then rest for 10 minutes.
4. Meanwhile place the other 1 oz (25 g) of fat and the sugar in a jug and melt together on High/600W for 60 seconds.
5. Roll the dough on a lightly floured surface to a rectangle measuring 12 × 9 inches (30 × 22.5 cm). Spread with the melted butter and sugar and then sprinkle the dried fruit and peel evenly over the top.
6. Roll up as you would a Swiss roll and cut into 9 equal pieces.
7. Line the base of a 7½ inch (19 cm) baking dish and lightly oil.
8. Place 7 pieces, cut side up, in a circle and the other two in the centre. All the pieces should be touching.
9. Prove in the oven on High/600W for 10 seconds and then leave to stand for 10 minutes.
10. Repeat twice, then bake on High/600W for 4.30 minutes. Turn on to a wire cooling tray. Peel the paper off the base and pat the base dry with absorbent kitchen paper. Turn right way up and leave to cool.
11. Glaze the top with clear honey while still hot and again before serving, if liked.

Combination cooking Bake at 400°F/200°C on Medium/360W for 5 minutes.

Malt Loaf

Serves 10
½ pint (300 ml) skimmed milk
2 oz (50 g) soft vegetable margarine
2 oz (50 g) molasses
2 oz (50 g) malt extract
10 oz (275 g) wholemeal flour
1 tsp baking powder
3 oz (75 g) raisins

1. Place the milk, margarine, molasses and malt extract in a jug and heat on High/600W for 2 minutes.
2. Sift the flour together with the baking powder and stir in the raisins. Pour the liquid on to the dry ingredients and combine well.
3. Line the base of a 1¼ pint (0.75 litre) loaf dish and lightly oil. Place the mixture in the dish and smooth the top.
4. Cook on Medium/360W for 13 minutes. Remove from the oven and leave to stand for 5 minutes then turn out on to a wire rack and peel off the paper. Pat the base and sides dry with absorbent kitchen paper.
5. The top has a nice glossy finish, but you can brush it with molasses or date syrup or malt extract for extra sheen if you like.

Combination cooking Bake at 325°F/165°C on Medium/360W for 10 minutes, followed by a further 4 minutes on conventional heat only.

Boston Brown 'Bread'

Although this is called bread it is really more like a tasty cake in texture and colour.

Serves 6
2 oz (50 g) rye flour
2 oz (50 g) corn/maize flour
2 oz (50 g) wholemeal flour
1 tsp bicarbonate of soda
4 oz (100 g) seeded raisins
¼ pint (150 ml) natural yoghurt
1 free-range egg
2 oz (50 g) date syrup or malt extract

1. Line the base of a terrine or baking dish about 9½ × 4½ inches (25 × 12.5 cm) and lightly oil.
2. Sift the flours and bicarbonate into a mixing bowl and stir in the raisins.
3. Lightly beat the egg, yoghurt and date syrup and add them to the flour

and dry ingredients to make a soft mixture. Place this in the prepared dish and smooth the top.
4. Bake on High/600W for 4 minutes. Remove from oven and leave to stand for 5 minutes before peeling off the paper and cooling on a wire tray.

Combination cooking Bake at 350°F/180°C on Medium/360W for 8 minutes.

CAKES

REMEMBER TO line the bases of cake dishes with greaseproof paper. You need not grease the dishes themselves unless the cake has very little fat in it.

Use deep dishes and do not fill more than two-thirds full with mixture. Smooth the top and bake on the shelf in the oven, or on a piece of microwave ware such as a tray or roasting rack, to allow for more even distribution of microwaves through the base of the dish and to prevent soggy, uncooked bottoms to the cakes.

Undercook rather than overcook. If the cake is overcooked it will be ruined – tough, rubbery and dry. If it is still underdone after the usual 5 minutes' standing time it can go back into the oven for a further 30 seconds. Very big cakes may need up to 15 minutes' standing time.

Raspberry Jam Buns

Makes 10
4 oz (100 g) self-raising wholemeal flour
2 oz (50 g) soft vegetable margarine
2 oz (50 g) light muscovado sugar
pinch sea salt
1 free-range egg (size 4)
no-added-sugar raspberry jam

1. Lightly oil or line a microwave tray.
2. Sift the flour into a mixing bowl and rub in the fat until the mixture resembles breadcrumbs in consistency.
3. Stir in the sugar, salt and lightly beaten egg to make a soft dough and roll into a long thick sausage, then cut into 10 pieces.
4. Take each piece and make an indentation with your thumb. Fill this with jam and pinch the top together over the jam.
5. Place on the prepared tray and bake on High/600W for 3.30 minutes.

Combination cooking Bake at 350°F/180°C on Medium/360W for 6 minutes.

Ground Coffee Cake

Serves 8
3 free-range eggs, separated
3 oz (75 g) light muscovado sugar
2 oz (50 g) soft vegetable margarine
1 oz (25 g) wholemeal semolina
2 oz (50 g) wholemeal flour
1 tsp baking powder
1 tbsp ground decaffeinated coffee
icing sugar to dust

1. Whisk the egg whites until stiff.
2. Whisk together the egg yolks and sugar until thick in consistency and pale in colour.
3. Place the margarine in a basin or jug and melt on High/600W for 20 seconds.
4. Sift the flour and semolina with the baking powder and ground coffee.
5. Stir the margarine into the egg and sugar mixture, then fold in the flour and pour into a lightly oiled savarin mould or ring-cake mould and bake on High/600W for 4 minutes. Stand for 5 minutes before inverting the dish, upon which the cake should gently come away from the sides.
6. Dust with a little icing sugar sieved on to the top of the cake.

Combination cooking Bake at 350°F/180°C on Medium/360W for 5 minutes.

Paper-Cup Madeleines

For important further details about microbaking in paperware see page xxv.

Makes 6
4 oz (100 g) soft vegetable margarine
3 oz (75 g) light muscovado sugar
1 free-range egg
4 oz (100 g) wholemeal flour
1 tsp baking powder
3 drops vanilla essence

To decorate
2 heaped tbsp no-added-sugar raspberry (or similar red) jam
2 tsp water
6 tbsp desiccated coconut

1. Cream together the margarine and sugar until the mixture is light and fluffy.
2. Lightly beat the egg and cream it into the mixture.

3. Sift the flour and baking powder and fold into the mixture together with the vanilla essence.

4. Divide the mixture between 6 paper cups and bake on Medium/360W for 6-7 minutes. Remove from the oven and turn the paper cups upside-down over a wire cooling tray. The cakes should drop out easily.

5. Place the jam and water in a small basin and heat on High/600W for 60 seconds. Remove and stir.

6. As soon as they are cool enough to handle, spoon the jam over the top and sides of the madeleines and roll them in the coconut. Leave until cold.

Combination cooking Bake at 375°F/190°C on Medium/360W for 6 minutes.

Turnpike Cake

Serves 8
8 oz (225 g) soft vegetable margarine
6 oz (175 g) dark muscovado sugar
2 tbsp date syrup
4 free-range eggs
6 oz (175 g) sultanas
6 oz (175 g) currants
3 oz (75 g) other dried fruit of choice (dates, peaches, apple rings)
-8 oz (225 g) wholemeal flour
2 tsp baking powder
2 tbsp brandy

To decorate
6 glacé cherries
some flaked almonds, lightly toasted

1. Line the base of a 7 inch (17.5 cm) cake dish.

2. Cream together the margarine and sugar until the mixture is light and fluffy in consistency. Beat in the date syrup.

3. Add the eggs one at a time, beating well in between.

4. Fold in the dried fruit and the sifted flour and baking powder then lightly beat in the brandy.

5. Place in the prepared dish and smooth the top. Halve the cherries and arrange on top with the nuts, pressing them lightly into the mixture.

6. Bake on Medium/360W for 7 minutes.

7. Remove from the oven and stand in the dish for 5 minutes. Turn out and peel the paper off the base, then allow to become cold on a wire cooling tray.

Combination cooking Bake at 350°F/180°C on Medium/360W for 6 minutes.

Farmhouse Cake

Serves 10
5 oz (150 g) soft vegetable margarine
3 oz (75 g) light muscovado sugar
2 oz (50 g) clear honey
2 free-range eggs
4 oz (100 g) raisins
4 oz (100 g) sultanas
8 oz (225 g) wholemeal flour
1 tsp baking powder
1 tbsp Demerara sugar

1. Line the base of a 7 inch (17.5 cm) cake dish.
2. Cream together the margarine, sugar and honey until light and fluffy in consistency.
3. Lightly beat the eggs and add, half at a time, to the mixture, adding a little flour if it shows signs of curdling.
4. Stir in the dried fruit.
5. Sift the flour and baking powder and fold into the mixture. Place in the prepared dish and smooth the top. Sprinkle over the Demerara sugar and bake on High/600W for 6 minutes.
6. Remove from the oven and leave to stand for 5 minutes before turning out of the dish. If you cool the cake upside-down on a wire rack it will receive an attractive patterned imprint on the top from the rack.

Combination cooking Bake at 350°F/180°C on Medium/360W for 8 minutes.

Gingerbread with Real Ginger

Serves 9
10 oz (275 g) wholemeal flour
2 tsp ground ginger
1 tsp bicarbonate of soda
3 oz (75 g) soft vegetable margarine
2 oz (50 g) light muscovado sugar
2 oz (50 g) molasses
¼ pint (150 ml) skimmed milk
1 tsp lemon juice
⅛ pint (75 ml) black decaffeinated coffee
1 tbsp stem ginger syrup
4 oz (100 g) raisins
1 oz (25 g) stem ginger, finely chopped
2 free-range eggs

1. Lightly oil and line the base of a 9 inch (22.5 cm) square dish.
2. Sift the flour, ginger and bicarbonate into a mixing bowl.
3. Place the margarine, sugar, molasses, milk, lemon juice, black coffee and ginger syrup in a jug or basin and melt on Medium/360W for 2 minutes. Remove and stir well.
4. Stir the raisins and stem ginger into the flour.
5. Lightly beat the eggs. Make a well in the flour and add the eggs, then gradually pour in the liquid, beating to make a thick batter.
6. Place the batter in the prepared dish and bake on Medium/360W for 10 minutes.
7. Remove from the oven and allow to stand in the dish for 5 minutes. Remove and peel paper off the base. Pat dry with absorbent kitchen paper, if necessary. Cut into squares when cold.

Combination cooking Bake at 350°F/180°C on Medium/360W for 8 minutes.

Coconut Hearts

Makes 8
4 oz (100 g) soft vegetable margarine
3 oz (75 g) fructose
1 free-range egg (size 2)
2 oz (50 g) wholemeal flour
1 tsp baking powder
1 oz (25 g) brown rice flour or wholemeal semolina
1 oz (25 g) desiccated coconut
1 free-range egg white

To decorate
2 heaped tbsp red no-added-sugar jam
2 oz (50 g) desiccated coconut

1. Prepare 8 ceramic *coeur à la crème* moulds by lining the bases with greaseproof paper. If you have only 4, bake in two batches.
2. Cream together the margarine and fructose until light and fluffy in consistency. Lightly beat the egg and add to the mixture.
3. Sift the flour and baking powder and mix with the rice flour and the 1 oz (25 g) of coconut.
4. Fold the flour mixture into the creamed mixture.
5. Whisk the egg white until it forms stiff peaks and then fold into the mixture. Fill the moulds two-thirds full and smooth the tops.
6. Bake on Medium/360W for 4 minutes if cooking four at a time, or for 5 minutes if cooking all eight, then on High/600W for a further 2.30 minutes for four, 3.30 minutes for eight. Move the ceramic moulds during the baking if the oven does not have a turntable, to ensure even cooking.

Passion Cake (page 42)

Remove from oven and pat tops with absorbent kitchen paper. Stand for 5 minutes before turning out. Don't forget to reline the base of the moulds if cooking in two batches.

7. While the cakes are still warm, spread the top and sides with a little jam and roll in the coconut.

Combination cooking Bake at 375°F/190°C on Medium/360W for 5 minutes if cooking in two batches, and for 8 minutes if cooking in a single batch.

Swiss Tarts

Makes 6
3 oz (75 g) soft vegetable margarine
1 oz (25 g) fructose
3 drops vanilla essence
3 oz (75 g) wholemeal flour
2 tbsp red no-added-sugar jam

1. Place 6 double baking cases (one inside the other) on the microwave tray or turntable. Have ready a piping bag fitted with a ½ inch (1.75 cm) star or noisette nozzle.
2. Cream together the margarine, fructose and vanilla essence until light and fluffy, then fold in the sifted flour to make a stiff paste.
3. Place in the piping bag and pipe whirls into the prepared baking cases, making a slight indent in the centre.
4. Bake on Low/180W for 5 minutes. Remove from the oven and cool on a baking tray.
5. When cold place a small blob of jam in the centre of each bun.

Combination cooking Bake at 325°F/160°C on Medium/360W for 3.30 minutes.

Fruit Slice

Serves 8-9
4 oz (100 g) stoned cooking dates
1 tbsp concentrated apple juice
3 tbsp water
4 oz (100 g) soft vegetable margarine
2 free-range eggs, lightly beaten
8 oz (225 g) wholemeal flour
1 tsp baking powder
½ tsp each ground cinnamon and mixed spice

Swiss Tarts and Fruit Slice (page 35), Coconut Hearts (page 34)

2 oz (50 g) dried apricots
3 oz (75 g) sultanas
3 oz (75 g) raisins

1. Line the base of a 9 inch (22.5 cm) dish.
2. Chop the dates into small pieces and place in a covered dish with the apple juice and water. Cook on High/600W for 3 minutes, stirring once or twice. Remove and mash with a fork to produce a smooth purée.
3. Cream the margarine and date purée.
4. Beat in the eggs.
5. Sift the flour, baking powder and spices into a mixing bowl.
6. Chop the apricots and stir them, together with the other dried fruit, into the flour mixture.
7. Fold the flour into the creamed mixture, place in the prepared dish and level the top.
8. Bake on High/600W for 7 minutes. Remove from oven and stand for 5 minutes, then invert and peel the paper off the base of the slice. Pat dry with a piece of absorbent kitchen paper.

Combination cooking Bake at 350°F/180°C on High/600W for 4 minutes.

Vanilla Fairy Cakes

Makes 8
2 oz (50 g) soft vegetable margarine
2 oz (50 g) light muscovado sugar
1 free-range egg, lightly beaten
2 drops natural vanilla essence
2 oz (50 g) wholemeal flour
½ tsp baking powder

1. Prepare 8 double paper baking cases (one case inside the other) on the microwave tray or turntable.
2. Cream together the margarine and sugar and beat in the egg and vanilla essence.
3. Sift the flour and baking powder and add to the mixture.
4. Spoon into the prepared cases and bake on High/600W for 3 minutes.
5. If liked, decorate with frosting.

Combination cooking Bake at 350°F/180°C on Medium/360W for 3 minutes.

Honey and Chocolate Cake

Serves 6-8
3 free-range eggs
8 oz (225 g) clear honey
7 oz (200 g) wholemeal flour
1 oz (25 g) cocoa or carob powder
1 tbsp Grand Marnier liqueur

1. Line the base of a 6 inch (15 cm) cake dish or a 2½ pint (1.5 litre) soufflé dish.
2. Whisk the eggs and honey in an electric mixer until they become thick and ropy and can support your initials drizzled on the top using the mixture.
3. Sift the flour and cocoa powder together and carefully fold into the mixture using a metal tablespoon. Add the Grand Marnier at the same time.
4. Bake on High/600W for 7 minutes, allow to stand for 5 minutes and if the centre is still a little moist bake for a further 60 seconds.
5. Cool on a wire tray before removing from the dish.

Combination cooking Bake at 350°F/180°C on Medium/360W for 5 minutes.

Banana Cake

Serves 8
4 oz (100 g) soft vegetable margarine
3½ oz (85 g) light muscovado sugar
1 free-range (size 2) egg, lightly beaten
2 small ripe bananas
5 oz (150 g) wholemeal flour
1 tsp baking powder

1. Line the base of a terrine or baking dish about 9 × 4 inches (22.5 × 10 cm).
2. Cream together the margarine and sugar until light and fluffy then beat in the egg, adding a little flour if the mixture looks like curdling.
3. Mash the bananas and beat into the mixture.
4. Sift the flour and baking powder and fold into the mixture, then place in the prepared dish and level the top.
5. Bake for 8 minutes on Medium/360W and cool slightly on a wire tray before removing from the dish.

Combination cooking Bake at 375°F/190°C on High/600W for 5 minutes.

Yoghurt Cake

Serves 8
4 oz (100 g) soft vegetable margarine
4 oz (100 g) clear honey
3 drops vanilla essence
1 free-range egg (size 1)
4 oz (100 g) Greek-style yoghurt
6 oz (175 g) wholemeal flour
1 tsp baking powder

Topping
4 oz (100 g) Greek-style yoghurt
2 tsp clear honey

1. Line the base of a 6 inch (15 cm) cake dish or a 2½ pint (1.5 litre) soufflé dish.
2. Cream together the margarine, honey and vanilla essence until pale in colour and of a soft dropping consistency.
3. Lightly beat the egg and cream into the mixture.
4. Add 4 oz (100 g) yoghurt.
5. Sift the flour and baking powder and fold into the mixture.
6. Spoon into the prepared dish and bake on High/600W for 8 minutes. Remove and leave to stand in the dish for 5 minutes before turning out to cool on a wire cooling tray.
7. When almost cold spread the remaining yoghurt over the top and then drizzle honey over the yoghurt. This layer will thicken if left overnight or until you are ready to serve the cake.

Combination cooking   Bake at 375°F/190°C on High/600W for 6 minutes.

Victoria Sandwich

Serves 8
6 oz (175 g) soft vegetable margarine
6 oz (175 g) light muscovado sugar
3 drops vanilla essence
2 free-range eggs (size 2)
6 oz (175 g) wholemeal flour
apricot no-added-sugar jam to sandwich

1. Line the bases of two 7½ inch (18.75cm) cake dishes.
2. Cream together the margarine, sugar and vanilla essence until pale in colour and of a soft dropping consistency.
3. Lightly beat the eggs and add one at a time.

4. Sift the flour and fold in. Divide the mixture between the two cake dishes, levelling the tops.

5. Bake one at a time, on High/600W, for 7 minutes each. Remove from the oven and leave in the dishes for 5 minutes. Remove and allow to become completely cold before sandwiching together with the jam.

6. Traditionally a little icing sugar or caster sugar is sprinkled on top of the sponge.

Combination cooking Bake at 350°F/180°C on High/600W for 5 minutes.

Rock Buns

Makes 12
8 oz (225 g) wholemeal flour
1 tsp baking powder
1 tsp mixed spice
3 oz (75 g) soft vegetable margarine
2 oz (50 g) sultanas
2 oz (50 g) currants
1 oz (25 g) Demerara sugar
1 free-range egg
2 tbsp skimmed milk

1. Line the microwave tray.

2. Sift the flour into a mixing bowl together with the baking powder and mixed spice.

3. Rub in the fat until the mixture resembles breadcrumbs in consistency. Stir in the dried fruit and sugar.

4. Lightly beat the egg and add to the mixture with the milk. Stir well to a softish consistency, then drop 6 large spoonfuls on to the paper and roughen the tops with a fork.

5. Bake on Medium/360W for 4 minutes. Bake the remainder.

Combination cooking Bake at 375°F/190°C on Medium/360W for 3.30 minutes.

Chocolate or Carob Celebration Cake

Serves 8
4 oz (100 g) plain chocolate or carob
1 tbsp decaffeinated coffee granules
1 tbsp water
4 oz (100 g) soft vegetable margarine
2 oz (50 g) dark muscovado sugar

2 oz (50 g) clear honey
3 free-range eggs
8 oz (225 g) wholemeal flour

Topping
2 oz (50 g) plain chocolate or carob
4 oz (100 g) low-fat curd cheese

1. Lightly oil a 2½ pint (1.5 litre) soufflé dish.
2. Break up the 4 oz (100 g) chocolate/carob into squares and place in a shallow dish with the coffee granules and water. Heat on High/600W for 1.30 minutes.
3. Cream together the margarine, sugar and honey until light and fluffy.
4. Lightly beat the eggs and gradually add them to the mixture.
5. Sift the flour and fold it in.
6. Spoon into the prepared dish and bake on High/600W for 6 minutes. Remove and leave to stand for 5 minutes before removing from the dish and cooling on a wire cooling tray.
7. When cold, make the topping by melting the 2 oz (50 g) chocolate/carob, as above, and mixing with the curd cheese.

Combination cooking Bake at 350°F/180°C on High/600W for 4.30 minutes.

Swiss Roll

Serves 6-8
3 oz (75 g) clear honey
3 free-range eggs
3 oz (75 g) wholemeal flour
1 tbsp boiling water

Suggested filling
4 oz (100 g) no-added-sugar black cherry or raspberry jam
6 oz (175 g) Greek-style yoghurt

1. To make a paper Swiss roll case, line a Swiss roll tin 11 × 7 inches (27.5 × 17.5 cm) with a double layer of greaseproof, baking or silicone baking paper. Shape the edges by cutting into the corners with scissors and then folding the edges around. Staple in place at each corner and then strengthen the edges with a layer of brown tape or masking tape. Lightly oil.
2. Whisk the honey and eggs together until pale in colour and thick and ropy in consistency.
3. Sift the flour and then fold first the water and then the flour into the eggs.

4. Pour into the prepared case, making it as level and evenly spread as possible. Bake on High/600W for 4.30 minutes.

5. Remove from the oven and cool for a minute, then invert on to a clean sheet of greaseproof paper. Peel off the paper case and trim the edges using a sharp knife. If you plan to use as soon as the cake is cool you can spread it with jam while it is hot. Otherwise you can roll up and cool on a wire cooling tray.

6. Unroll and fill with a layer of jam topped with yoghurt, or other filling of your choice. This will freeze well unfilled. Thaw and fill as desired.

Combination cooking Bake at 375°F/190°C on High/600W for 3.30 minutes.

Note So far no microwave manufacturers make a Swiss roll dish, so Step 1 above shows you how to make your own.

Battenberg

Serves 8-10
6 oz (175 g) soft vegetable margarine
4 oz (100 g) light muscovado sugar
2 free-range eggs
1 oz (25 g) cocoa or carob powder
3 tbsp boiling water
6½ oz (190 g) wholemeal flour
2 drops vanilla essence
apricot jam or spread
8-9 oz (225-250 g) block white or raw cane sugar marzipan

1. Lightly oil and line the base of a 1¼ pint (0.75 litre) loaf dish.

2. Beat the margarine and sugar until pale in colour and light and fluffy in consistency. Gradually beat in the eggs, being careful not to curdle the mixture. Remove half the mixture and place in another bowl.

3. Mix the cocoa powder and water together to make a paste. Stir into one half of the cake mixture and fold in half the sifted flour. Add the vanilla essence and the rest of the flour to the other half of the cake mixture.

4. Place one of the prepared mixtures in the dish and level the top. Bake on Medium/360W for 3.30 minutes. Remove from oven and lift out of dish, leaving to cool in the paper on a wire cooling tray. Reline the dish and bake the second half as before.

5. When the cakes are cold, place one half on top of the other and cut through lengthways to make the four fingers of the Battenberg. Arrange with the two vanilla and two chocolate quarters diagonally opposite each other and sandwich them in place with a little apricot spread or jam. Spread the outside of the cake with jam ready to receive the marzipan.

6. Place the marzipan in the microwave on High/600W for 30 seconds to soften. Roll out on a lightly floured board and then wrap around the cake. Trim each end of the cake.

Combination cooking Bake at 350°F/180°C on Medium/360W for 3 minutes.

No-Added-Sugar Fruit Cake

Serves 8
4 oz (100 g) cooking dates, pitted and chopped
4 tbsp water
2 tbsp concentrated apple juice
8 oz (225 g) wholemeal flour
1 tsp baking powder
½ tsp each ground cinnamon and mixed spice
4 oz (100 g) soft vegetable margarine
2 oz (50 g) dried apricots, finely diced
3 oz (75 g) sultanas, finely diced
3 oz (75 g) raisins, finely diced
2 free-range eggs, lightly beaten

1. Place the dates and apple juice in a dish with the water and cover with a lid. Cook on High/600W for 4 minutes, stirring twice during the cooking to help break up the dates to a purée. Remove and mash or liquidize.
2. Sift the flour and baking powder into a mixing bowl together with the spices, and rub in the margarine. Stir in the dried fruits.
3. Beat in the eggs and then the date purée and spoon into a lightly oiled cake dish of about 8 inches (20 cm). Smooth the top and bake on High/600W for 7 minutes.
4. Remove from oven and leave to stand in the dish for 5 minutes before turning out and patting the base and sides dry with absorbent kitchen paper.
5. Invert and leave to cool (or eat hot with custard as a pudding!)

Combination cooking Bake at 350°F/180°C on Medium/360W for 11 minutes.

Passion Cake

Serves 8
4 oz (100 g) clear honey
6 oz (175 g) soft vegetable margarine
3 free-range eggs
6 oz (175 g) grated carrot

4 oz (100 g) diced walnut pieces
8 oz (225 g) wholemeal flour
1 tsp baking powder

Frosting
8 oz (225 g) low-fat curd cheese
4 oz (100 g) Greek-style yoghurt
4 tbsp concentrated apple juice

1. Line the base of an 8 inch (20 cm) cake dish.
2. Cream together the honey and margarine until light in colour and fluffy in consistency.
3. Lightly beat the eggs and add them one at a time to the mixture.
4. Carefully fold in the carrots and walnuts.
5. Sift the flour and baking powder together and fold into the mixture.
6. Place in the dish, level the top, and bake on High/600W for 6 minutes.
7. Remove from the oven and stand for 5 minutes before inverting and peeling off the paper, then reinverting and allowing to become completely cold before frosting.
8. Mix together the frosting ingredients and spread over the top of the cake, roughing up with a fork.

Combination cooking Bake at 350°F/180°C on High/600W for 6 minutes, followed by 4 minutes on conventional heat only.

Plain Gingerbread

Serves about 9
⅓ pint (200 ml) skimmed milk
4 oz (100 g) soft vegetable margarine
4 oz (100 g) clear honey
4 oz (100 g) molasses
10 oz (275 g) wholemeal flour
1 tsp baking powder
2 tsp ground ginger
1 tsp ground cinnamon
1 free-range egg, lightly beaten

1. Line the base of a 7 inch (17.5 cm) cake dish.
2. Measure the milk into a measuring jug and then add the margarine, honey and molasses and melt together on High/600W for 2 minutes, stirring once during the cooking.
3. Sift the flour and spices into a mixing bowl and make a well in the centre. Add the egg and the liquid and combine thoroughly with a wooden spoon.
4. Place in the dish and bake for 13 minutes on Medium/360W.

5. Remove from the oven and allow to stand in the dish for 5 minutes before turning out on to a wire cooling rack.
6. The top has a nice glossy finish, but you can brush it with molasses or date syrup or malt extract for extra sheen if you like.

Combination cooking Bake at 325°F/165°C on Medium/360W for 13 minutes, followed by a further 4 minutes on conventional heat only.

Cherry and Coconut Cake

Serves 8
12 oz (325 g) wholemeal flour
1 tsp baking powder
5 oz (150 g) soft vegetable margarine
4 oz (100 g) glacé cherries
2 oz (50 g) desiccated coconut
3 oz (75 g) light muscovado sugar
2 free-range eggs
⅛ pint (75 ml) skimmed milk
glacé cherries, or coconut and jam to decorate

1. Line the base of a 7 inch (17.5 cm) cake or soufflé dish.
2. Sift the flour into a mixing bowl together with the baking powder. Rub in the fat until the mixture resembles breadcrumbs in consistency.
3. Chop the cherries and then stir them, with the coconut and the sugar, into the flour.
4. Lightly beat the eggs and milk together and beat into the flour mixture.
5. Place in the dish and bake on High/600W for 6 minutes.
6. Leave to stand in the dish for 5 minutes before turning out and cooling on a wire rack.
7. Decorate the top with cherry halves or spread the sides with jam and then dust with coconut, if liked.

Combination cooking Bake at 375°F/190°C on Medium/360W for 8 minutes.

DESSERTS

MICROBAKING CAN contribute to a huge range of attractive desserts including gâteaux, cakes, cheesecakes, mousses and old-fashioned favourites like pies and Bakewell tarts.

Several desserts require pastry cases that are baked blind, which means baked without a filling. To bake blind in a microwave oven:
1. Lightly oil the dish and line with the pastry.
2. Prick the pastry and place a layer of greaseproof, baking or silicone baking paper on top of the pastry.
3. Place a plate or some baking beans on top of the paper to weigh the pastry down.
4. Bake on High/600W for 2 minutes.
5. Remove the plate/beans and paper and bake for another 30 seconds, or if the case is to be used without further cooking for another 1.30 minutes.

Combination cooking Proceed as for microbaking then cook at 400°F/200°C on High/600W for 2 minutes. Remove the plate/beans and paper and cook for a further 60 seconds.

Pecan and Maple Syrup Pie

Serves 6-8

Pastry
4 oz (100 g) wholemeal flour
3 oz (75 g) soft vegetable margarine
2 oz (50 g) ground pecan nuts
cold water to mix

Filling
1 oz (25 g) soft vegetable margarine
6 oz (175 g) maple syrup
2 oz (50 g) golden syrup
1 free-range egg
2 oz (50 g) wholemeal breadcrumbs
6 oz (175 g) pecan halves

1. Lightly oil a 7 inch (17.5 cm) dish.
2. Sift the flour into a mixing bowl and rub in the fat until the mixture resembles breadcrumbs in consistency.
3. Stir in the ground pecans and mix in enough cold water to make a soft dough.
4. Roll out on a lightly floured board, and line the prepared dish. Bake blind. (Here and in following recipes, for baking blind see above).
5. Place the fat and the syrups in a jug and warm together in the oven on Medium/360W until dissolved. Cool slightly then add the lightly beaten egg.

6. Place the breadcrumbs in the base of the prepared pastry case and arrange the pecan halves attractively on top, then pour over the syrup mixture. Bake on High/600W for 5 minutes. Remove and rest for 5 minutes then return for a further 3 minutes.

Combination cooking Bake the filled pastry case at 375°F/190°C on High/600W for 7 minutes.

Pear Franzipan

Serves 8

Pastry
4 oz (100 g) wholemeal flour
2 oz (50 g) ground almonds
3 oz (75 g) soft vegetable margarine
½ free-range egg to bind

Filling
3 pears
4 oz (100 g) soft vegetable margarine
4 oz (100 g) light muscovado sugar
1½ free-range eggs
2 oz (50 g) ground almonds
4 oz (100 g) wholemeal flour
apricot spread or no-added-sugar jam

1. Lightly oil an 8 inch (20 cm) flan dish.
2. Sift the flour into a mixing bowl and stir in the almonds. Rub in the fat until the mixture resembles breadcrumbs in consistency, then bind with the egg to make a soft dough.
3. Roll out on a lightly floured surface and line the dish with the pastry. Bake blind.
4. Halve and core the pears – they do not have to be peeled – and cook in a little water on High/600W in a covered dish for 3 minutes. Remove and allow to cool while you make the filling.
5. Cream together the margarine and sugar until pale in colour and of a soft dropping consistency. Beat in the egs, then add the almonds and fold in the flour.
6. Place the pears in the pastry case, cut side down. Top with the franzipan mixture and bake on High/600W for 4.30 minutes.
7. While still hot brush the top with the spread or jam.

Combination cooking Bake the filled pastry case at 375°F/190°C on Medium/360W for 8 minutes.

Guava and Raspberry Gâteau

This is an impressive dessert. Sandwiched between two light layers of sponge is a layer of guava mousse and whole raspberries. The gâteau is then coated in a red glaze through which you can see the layers of mousse filling and sponge.

Serves 8

Sponge
2 free-range eggs
3 oz (75 g) clear honey
2 drops of almond essence
2 oz (50 g) wholemeal flour
3 oz (75 g) ground almonds

Filling
2 guavas
¼ pint (150 ml) tropical or exotic mixed fruit juice
3 tsp gelatine
8 oz (225 g) Greek-style yoghurt
⅓ pint (200 ml) crème fraîche or soured cream
8 oz (225 g) whole raspberries, fresh or thawed

Glaze
2 tsp gelatine
4 tbsp boiling water
¼ pint (150 ml) red fruit juice of choice

1. Line the bases of two 6 inch (15 cm) cake dishes.
2. Whisk the eggs and honey together until pale in colour and thick and ropy in consistency.
3. Add the essence, then fold in the flour and almonds and pour into the dishes. Cook each separately on Medium/360W for 3.30 minutes. Leave to stand in the dishes for 3 minutes then turn out to cool.
4. To make the filling, peel and quarter the guavas. Place in a dish with a lid in about 1 inch (2.5 cm) of water. Cover and cook on High/600W for 3 minutes. Drain, and using a wooden spoon press through a sieve. It does take a little while to get all the flesh separated from the pips, which you can discard.
5. Place the fruit juice in a jug or cup and sprinkle on the gelatine. Place in the microwave on High/600W for 1.30 minutes, then stir to ensure the gelatine is completely dissolved. Place on one side.
6. Place the yoghurt and crème fraîche in a mixing bowl and blend with the guava purée, gelatine and fruit juice. Stir well and leave the mousse in the fridge or freezer until on the point of setting.
7. To assemble the gâteau, line the base and sides of a soufflé dish having

the same diameter as the sponge cakes. Place one layer of sponge in the base. Top with the raspberries.

8. Pour over the mousse. Top with the second sponge layer and pat lightly in place. Leave in the fridge for at least 2 hours to set.

9. Place a plate or serving dish over the base of the soufflé dish and invert. Peel off the paper.

10. Towards the end of the 2 hours, sprinkle the 2 tsp gelatine on to the water and stir to dissolve. Stir into the red fruit juice and leave to cool.

11. When on the point of setting – about 25 minutes – spoon over the top and sides of the turned-out gâteau.

Combination cooking Bake at 350°F/180°C on Medium/360W for 4 minutes.

Pumpkin Pie

Serves 8

Pastry
6 oz (175 g) wholemeal flour
3 oz (75 g) soft vegetable margarine
skimmed milk to mix

Filling
1 lb (450 g) pumpkin
4 tbsp water
2 free-range eggs
4 tbsp skimmed milk
2 tbsp clear honey
freshly grated nutmeg

1. Lightly oil an 8 inch (20 cm) serving dish.

2. Sift the flour into a mixing bowl and rub in the margarine until the mixture resembles breadcrumbs in consistency.

3. Mix to a soft dough with the milk, roll out on a lightly floured surface, and bake blind in the prepared dish.

4. Peel and chop the pumpkin and place in a dish with a lid, together with the water. Cover and cook on High/600W for 6-8 minutes until the pumpkin is soft. Drain, if necessary, and purée in a blender or liquidizer.

5. Blend the eggs, milk and honey into the purée and pour into the pastry case. Top with freshly grated nutmeg and bake on Medium/360W for 5 minutes. Stand for 5 minutes, then bake for another 5 minutes. Remove and cool.

Combination cooking Bake the filled pastry case at 350°F/180°C on Medium/360W for 7 minutes.

Guava Cheesecake

Serves 8

Pastry
6 oz (175 g) wholemeal flour
4 oz (100 g) soft vegetable margarine
2 drops vanilla essence
3 tbsp skimmed milk

Filling
3 guavas
2 tbsp water
8 oz (225 g) low-fat curd cheese
8 oz (225 g) Greek-style yoghurt
2 free-range eggs, separated
2 tbsp clear honey

1. Lightly oil an 8 inch (20 cm) serving dish.
2. Sift the flour into a mixing bowl and rub in the fat until the mixture resembles breadcrumbs in consistency.
3. Add the vanilla essence and mix to a soft dough with the milk. Roll out and bake blind in the prepared dish.
4. Peel and quarter the guavas and place in a dish with a lid, together with the water. Cover and cook on High/600W for 4-5 minutes.
5. Drain the guavas and then sieve them.
6. Mix the guava purée with the cheese, yoghurt, egg yolks and honey.
7. Whisk the egg whites until stiff and fold into the mixture. Pour into the pastry case and bake on Medium/360W for 10 minutes.
8. Remove and stand for 5 minutes. Turn out and cool before serving.

Combination cooking Bake at 350°F/180°C on Medium/360W for 7 minutes.

Chocolate Mousse Gâteau

Serves 8

Sponge
3 free-range eggs
3½ oz (90 g) dark muscovado sugar
1 tsp decaffeinated coffee granules
2 tbsp boiling water
3 oz (75 g) wholemeal flour
1 oz (25 g) cocoa or carob powder

Pecan and Maple Syrup Pie (page 46) and Pear Franzipan (page 47)

Mousse
3 tsp gelatine
4 tbsp boiling water
⅛ pint (75 ml) decaffeinated black coffee
4 oz (100 g) plain dark chocolate or carob
8 oz (225 g) Greek-style yoghurt
5 oz (150 ml) double cream

1. Whisk together the eggs and sugar in an electric mixer until pale in colour and thick and ropy in consistency.
2. Dissolve the coffee granules in the 2 tbsp boiling water and add to the mixture.
3. Sift together the flour and cocoa powder or carob and fold into the mixture.
4. Divide between two 6 inch (15 cm) cake dishes and bake each separately on Medium/360W for 4 minutes. Turn out to cool on a wire cooling tray. When cold, slice one of the cakes in half horizontally.
5. To make the mousse, sprinkle the gelatine on to the water and stir to dissolve. Add the coffee and leave to cool.
6. Break the chocolate or carob into squares and place in a shallow dish in the microwave on High/600W for 60 seconds. Remove and stir in the yoghurt.
7. Lightly whip the cream and fold in, together with the gelatine.
8. To assemble the gâteau, line the base and sides of a 6 inch (15 cm) soufflé dish and place one of the thinner layers of cake in the base.
9. Top with half the mousse. Place a second thin layer of cake on top. Add the rest of the mousse and lightly pat the thicker cake on top of that.
10. Leave in the fridge to set for at least an hour.
11. To serve, place a serving dish over the soufflé dish, invert to turn out and peel off the paper.

Combination cooking Bake each cake separately at 350°F/180°C on Medium/360W for 3.30 minutes.

Bread Pudding

Serves 8
5 oz (150 g) wholemeal bread
¼ pint (150 ml) skimmed milk
2 oz (50 g) soft vegetable margarine
2 oz (50 g) clear honey
4 oz (100 g) mixed dried fruit
2 free-range eggs

Guava and Raspberry Gâteau (page 48)

1. Lightly oil a 7 inch (17.5 cm) dish.
2. Break up the bread and soak it in the milk for a minimum of 30 minutes, then mash.
3. Melt the fat and honey on High/600W for 1.30 minutes and beat in with the soaked bread.
4. Add the dried fruit.
5. Beat the eggs lightly and add to the mixture.
6. Pour into the dish and bake on Medium/360W for 8 minutes. Leave to stand for 5 minutes and then return to the oven for a further 2-3 minutes.

Combination cooking Bake at 375°F/190°C on High/360W for 7 minutes.

Apple and Raspberry Marzipan Pies

Makes 8

Filling
2 oz (50 g) raw cane sugar marzipan
6 oz (175 g) apple
6 oz (175 g) raspberries

Pastry
6 oz (175 g) wholemeal flour
2 oz (50 g) ground almonds
4 oz (100 g) soft vegetable margarine
cold water to mix
egg white to glaze

1. Lightly oil an 8 cup bun tray.
2. Dice the marzipan and apple and pick over and hull the raspberries, if necessary. Place them all together in a dish with a lid and cook on High/600W for 3 minutes, stirring after 1.30 minutes.
3. Make the pastry by sieving the flour into a mixing bowl and stirring in the almonds. Rub in the fat until the mixture resembles breadcrumbs in consistency.
4. Bind together to form a soft dough with a little water and roll out. Using a scone or biscuit cutter cut out bases and lids for the bun tray.
5. Put the bases in place and fill with the raspberry mixture. Top each with a lid and glaze with egg white.
6. Bake on High/600W for 4 minutes. Reglaze and pop under a hot grill, if liked.

Combination cooking Bake at 400°F/200°C on High/600W for 3.30 minutes.

Patissier's Tart

This is a delicious pastry case filled with a layer of confectioner's custard and topped with two colourful fruits which are glazed with a fruit jelly. Slightly complicated, but don't be put off if you have the time.

Serves 8

Rich pastry
4 oz (100 g) self-raising wholemeal flour
4 oz (100 g) ground almonds
1 oz (25 g) dark muscovado sugar
5 oz (150 g) soft vegetable margarine
½ free-range egg to bind

Confectioner's custard
2 tsp gelatine
8 tbsp water
½ pint (300 ml) skimmed milk
1 oz (25 g) fructose
2 free-range eggs
2 drops vanilla essence
¼ pint (150 ml) red fruit juice

Fruit layer
1 lb (450 g) gooseberries
8 oz (225 g) raspberries, fresh or thawed

1. Place the topped and tailed gooseberries in a dish with a lid, with enough water to come half-way up them, and poach on Medium/360W for 5 minutes, stirring gently from time to time so as not to break the fruit. Leave to cool.
2. Lightly oil a 7½ inch (18.75 cm) flan dish.
3. Sift the flour into a mixing bowl and stir in the almonds and sugar. Rub in the fat until the mixture resembles breadcrumbs in consistency, then bind together with the egg to form a soft paste.
4. Roll out this rich pastry to line the dish. It is very soft, so you might find it easier to line the dish with the pastry in two halves. Because of its softness it can be pressed to join where breaks occur.
5. Bake blind in the usual way, except that after removing the plate and paper the pastry should be patted back into shape up the sides of the dish before it is returned to the oven for a further 1.30 minutes.
6. To make the custard, first sprinkle the gelatine on to the water in a container and heat on High/600W for 60 seconds to dissolve. Remove from the oven and leave half to cool. Stir the other half into the red fruit juice and leave this to cool and set (it will be used to glaze the top of the tart).

7. Place the milk and fructose in a jug and warm on High/600W for 1.30 minutes. Remove from the oven.

8. Lightly beat the eggs in a basin and pour on the hot milk and fructose, whisking with a fork as you do so.

9. Return to the jug through a sieve and cook on High/600W for about four 30 second bursts, stirring after each until the custard thickens (but do not overheat or it will curdle).

10. Add the vanilla essence and the gelatine mixture and leave to set. When on the point of setting, pour into the pastry case.

11. Arrange the prepared fruit on top in alternate sections and then glaze with the jelly when this is on the point of setting.

Bakewell Tart

Serves 6-8

Pastry
6 oz (175 g) wholemeal flour
2½ oz (65 g) soft vegetable margarine
cold water to mix

Filling
4 oz (100 g) soft vegetable margarine
4 oz (100 g) light muscovado sugar
2 free-range eggs
2 drops natural almond essence
4 oz (100 g) wholemeal flour
no-added-sugar jam for the base

1. Lightly oil a 7 inch (17.5 cm) flan dish.

2. To make the pastry, sift the flour into a mixing bowl and rub in the fat until the mixture resembles breadcrumbs in consistency.

3. Mix in the cold water to make a soft dough, then roll out and bake blind in the prepared dish. Any pastry scraps can be used to make a lattice-work top for the tart.

4. To make the filling, cream together the margarine and sugar until light and fluffy in consistency.

5. Beat in the eggs, one at a time, and the almond essence, adding a little flour if the mixture shows signs of curdling. Then fold in the sifted flour.

6. Place a layer of jam on the pastry and top with the sponge mixture. At this stage you can make a decorative lattice of pastry.

7. Bake on High/600W for 7 minutes. Glaze the top, when hot, by brushing with a little more jam.

Combination cooking Bake the filled pastry case at 400°F/200°C on Medium/360W for 8 minutes.

Lemon Curd Pie

Serves 8

Lemon curd
8 oz (225 g) light muscovado sugar
4 oz (100 g) unsalted butter
2 lemons, juice and grated rind
3 free-range eggs

Pastry
10 oz (275 g) wholemeal flour
6 oz (175 g) soft vegetable margarine
2 oz (50 g) ground almonds
2 oz (50 g) wholemeal semolina or brown rice flour
2 oz (50 g) light muscovado sugar
2 drops natural lemon oil

1. Place the sugar, butter and lemon juice and rind in a jug and heat on Medium/360W for 5 minutes. (To get more juice from the lemons, heat them on High/600W for 60 seconds before cutting and squeezing.) Remove and stir, then stand for 2 minutes.
2. Add the beaten eggs and mix well with a fork.
3. Return to the oven on Medium/360W for 8-9 minutes, stirring at one-minute intervals until the curd thickens. It is important to keep removing and stirring the mixture so that it does not curdle.
4. Lightly oil an 8 inch (20 cm) flan dish.
5. Sift the flour into a mixing bowl and rub in the fat until the mixture resembles breadcrumbs in consistency.
6. Stir in the almonds, semolina, sugar and oil and work to a soft dough with your hands.
7. Divide the pastry into two, roll out on a lightly floured surface, and line the base of the dish with half of it. The pastry is very rich and short so it will crumble easily, but do not be put off because it can be pressed together where it has cracked.
8. Fill with the lemon curd and top with a pastry lid. Bake on High/600W for 6-7 minutes. Allow to cool, and even chill if liked, before serving.

Combination cooking Bake the filled pastry case at 350°F/180°C on Medium/360W for 8 minutes.

Passion Fruit Gâteau

This gâteau looks very professional with a light and fluffy layer of mousse sandwiched between three layers of cake. The cake is then glazed with a light golden passion fruit gel, through which you can see the layers.

Serves 6

Sponge
3½ oz (87 g) wholemeal flour
1 oz (25 g) cornflour
3 free-range eggs (size 2)
4 oz (100 g) clear honey
2 drops natural vanilla essence

Mousse
⅛ pint (75 ml) tropical or exotic mixed fruit juice
3 tsp gelatine
6 passion fruit
8 oz (225 g) Greek-style yoghurt
⅓ pint (200 ml) crème fraîche or soured cream

Glaze
4 fl. oz (120 ml) tropical fruit juice
2 tsp gelatine
strained juice of 2 passion fruit

1. Lightly oil and line the base of two 6 inch (15 cm) cake or soufflé dishes.
2. Sift the flour and cornflour into a bowl.
3. Whisk the eggs and honey together in an electric mixer until pale, thick and ropy – the consistency should be such that it can support your initials drizzled on the top from the whisk. (If you do not have a mixer, whisk in a basin over a pan of boiling water.)
4. Add the vanilla essence and, quickly but carefully, fold in the flour using a metal tablespoon. Make sure you fold in all the flour, including that which falls to the base of the bowl.
5. Pour the mixture into the prepared dishes and bake separately on Medium/360W for 4 minutes. Remove and place on a wire cooling tray for 5 minutes, then turn out and if necessary pat the bases dry with a piece of absorbent kitchen paper. When cold slice one of the cakes horizontally into two layers.
6. To make the mousse, measure the fruit juice into a microwave ovenproof jug and sprinkle on the gelatine. Stir and heat on High/600W for 60 seconds until it is dissolved and the fruit juice is transparent. Leave to cool (you can speed this in the freezer – about 10 minutes – if you are careful not to let it set).
7. Scoop the centre from the passion fruit into a bowl and blend with the yoghurt and crème fraîche.
8. Whisk the egg whites until they form stiff peaks. Thoroughly fold in the gelatine and then the egg whites using a metal tablespoon.
9. For the glaze, sprinkle the 2 tsp gelatine on to the fruit juice and heat on High/600W for 60 seconds to dissolve.

10. Remove and add the strained juice of the passion fruit. Leave to cool.
11. To assemble, line the base and sides of a soufflé dish and place one of the thinner layers of cake in the base.
12. Top with half the mousse and place another thin layer of cake on top. Repeat with the second sponge layer and place in the fridge for a couple of hours to set.
13. Invert on to a serving dish or plate and peel off the paper, then spoon over the glaze when it is on the point of setting.

Combination cooking Bake each cake at 350°F/180°C on Medium/360W for 3 minutes.

Chocolate Gâteau

Serves 6

Sponge
2 free-range eggs
3 oz (75 g) clear honey
¼ pint (150 ml) water
4 oz (100 g) plain chocolate or carob
5 oz (150 g) wholemeal flour

Filling and topping
4 oz (100 g) plain chocolate or carob
8 oz (225 g) Greek-style yoghurt
14 oz (400 g) can black cherries

1. Lightly oil two 6 inch (15 cm) cake or soufflé dishes and line the bases.
2. Whisk the eggs and honey together in an electric cake-mixer until pale, thick and ropy – the consistency should be such that it can support your initials drizzled on the top from the whisk.
3. Place the water and chocolate in a basin or jug and microwave on High/600W for 1.30 minutes. Remove and stir the melted mixture together.
4. Add the chocolate to the eggs and honey and mix in well, then carefully fold in the sifted flour using a metal tablespoon.
5. Pour the mixture into the prepared dishes and bake together on Medium/360W for 5 minutes.
6. Allow to stand for a further 5 minutes before removing from the dishes and peeling off the paper.
7. To make the filling melt the chocolate in a basin on High/600W for 1.30 minutes and stir into the yoghurt.
8. When the cakes are cold sandwich together with a little of the filling and the stoned cherries and spread the remainder of the chocolate mixture on top.

Combination cooking Bake at 350°F/180°C on Medium/360W for 5 minutes.

Marzipan Apple Bake

Serves 4
1 lb (450 g) cooking apples
1 lemon, juice of
5 oz (150 g) marzipan, grated

Topping
8 oz (225 g) wholemeal flour
4 oz (100 g) soft vegetable margarine
2 oz (50 g) Demerara sugar

1. Wash, core and slice the apples – you don't have to peel them – and toss at once in the lemon juice to prevent discolouration.
2. Place the apples and lemon juice in a dish with a lid and cook on High/600W for 5 minutes, stirring to ensure even cooking. Remove from the oven, stir in the marzipan reserving 2 tbsp, and place in the bottom of a 2½ pint (1.5 litre) soufflé dish.
4. Sift the flour into a mixing bowl and rub in the fat until the mixture resembles breadcrumbs in consistency.
5. Stir in the sugar and the remainder of the marzipan, place the topping on the apple mixture and bake on Medium/360W for 8 minutes.

Combination cooking Bake at 400°F/200°C on Medium/360W for 5 minutes.

Apple Strudel

Serves 6-8
4 sheets filo pastry
½ oz (12 g) unsalted butter
2 oz (50 g) wholemeal breadcrumbs
1 lb (450 g) cooking apples
½ lemon, juice of
2 oz (50 g) sultanas
2 tbsp concentrated apple juice
1 tsp cinnamon
2 tbsp water
2 oz (50 g) chopped walnuts
2 tbsp no-added-sugar marmalade
½ oz (12 g) unsalted butter

1. Lightly oil a microwave shelf or tray.
2. Defrost the filo pastry, if necessary, and place 4 sheets on top of each other on the tray.
3. Fry the breadcrumbs in the butter until golden brown.
4. Peel, core and slice the apples, tossing in the lemon juice to prevent browning. Place them in a dish with a lid together with the sultanas, the apple juice, cinnamon and water and cook on High/600W for 2 minutes.
5. Drain the apples and mix with the nuts and breadcrumbs, spread the marmalade across the pastry and place the filling towards one edge of the pastry sheets. Tuck in the ends and then roll up in Swiss roll fashion.
6. Bake on High/600W for 6 minutes.
7. Remove from oven and, if liked, brush with the remaining butter and place under the grill to brown – be careful not to burn the top.

Combination cooking Glaze with eggwash and bake at 400°F/200°C on Medium/360W for 5 minutes.

Coffee and Chestnut Roulade

Serves 4

Sponge
3 free-range eggs
3 oz (75 g) light muscovado sugar
2 tbsp decaffeinated black coffee
3½ oz (90 g) wholemeal flour

Filling
1 tbsp decaffeinated black coffee
4 oz (100 g) Greek-style yoghurt
2 tbsp maple syrup
4 oz (100 g) chestnut purée

1. Make a paper Swiss roll case by lining a conventional Swiss roll tin with a double sheet of greaseproof, baking or silicone baking paper. Shape the edges by cutting into the corners and then folding them round. Staple into position and strengthen the edges with brown tape or masking tape. Lightly oil.
2. Whisk the eggs and sugar in an electric mixer until the volume has increased and the mixture is stiff enough to support your initials when drizzled on the top.
3. Fold in the coffee and the sieved flour. Place in the paper case, tilting to smooth the top.
4. Bake on High/600W for 4.30 minutes. Remove from the oven and pat the top dry, if necessary, with absorbent kitchen paper.
5. Invert on to a clean piece of greaseproof paper and carefully peel off the

paper case in which the roll was baked. Trim the edges, and roll up with the clean paper inside.

6. Place the filling ingredients in a blender and blend to a smooth purée.

7. When the cake is cold, unroll, remove the paper and fill. Roll up again. (Do not fill until shortly before use, or the roulade will become soggy.)

Combination cooking Bake at 375°C/190°F on Medium/360W for 5-6 minutes.

Pear Biscotte

Serves 6

6 oz (175 g) dried pears
4 oz (100 g) wholemeal flour
2 oz (50 g) soft vegetable margarine
2 oz (50 g) light muscovado sugar
1 free-range egg

1. Lightly oil the microwave shelf or turntable, or a flat baking dish about 7 inches (17.5 cm) in diameter.

2. Soak the pears overnight in boiling water, or cook with 4 tbsp water in a dish with a lid on High/600W for 4 minutes, stirring once. Mash or liquidize with a little of the cooking/soaking water to make a thickish purée.

3. Sift the flour into a mixing bowl. Rub in the fat until the mixture resembles breadcrumbs in consistency, then stir in the sugar.

4. Lightly beat the egg and add to the mixture to make a soft dough. Roll into a ball, wrap in greaseproof paper and chill for 30 minutes.

5. After removing from the fridge, roll out two 7 inch (17.5 cm) circles of dough. Place one on the prepared dish/tray and spread with the pear mixture. Top with the second circle. Bake for 5 minutes on High/600W.

Combination cooking Bake at 350°F/180°C on Medium/360W for 9 minutes.

Tarte Tatin

Serves 4

Pastry
2 oz (50 g) wholemeal flour
2 oz (50 g) ground almonds
2 oz (50 g) soft vegetable margarine
1 free-range egg yolk
cold water to mix

Topping
1½ oz (40 g) dark muscovado sugar
1 lb (450 g) dessert apples
½ lemon, juice of

1. Line the base of a small 6 inch (15 cm) cake dish and sprinkle with the sugar.
2. Sift the flour into a mixing bowl and stir in the ground almonds. Rub in the fat until the mixture resembles breadcrumbs in consistency.
3. Beat the egg yolk with a little water, add to the flour and mix to a soft dough. Roll out to fit the circumference of the dish.
4. Peel, core and slice the apples, tossing in lemon juice to prevent browning.
5. Arrange the apples in the dish on top of the sugar. Place the pastry on top and press lightly into position.
6. Bake on High/600W for 5 minutes. Remove from the oven and invert to serve. Make shortly before serving – if made too far in advance the dish will become soggy.

Combination cooking Bake at 400°F/200°C on High/600W for 4 minutes.

Baked Orange Cheesecake

Serves 6-8

Pastry
6 oz (175 g) wholemeal flour
3 oz (75 g) soft vegetable margarine
cold water to mix

Filling
8 oz (225 g) curd cheese
1 orange, juice and rind
2 free-range eggs, separated
2 tbsp clear honey
2 tbsp Greek-style yoghurt
2 oz (50 g) raisins

1. Line the base of a 7 inch (18.5 cm) dish.
2. Sift the flour into a mixing bowl, and rub in the fat until the mixture resembles breadcrumbs in consistency.
3. Bind to a soft dough with a little water, roll out and bake blind in the prepared dish.
4. Cream together the cheese, orange juice and rind, egg yolks, honey and yoghurt. Beat well and stir in the raisins.
5. Whisk the egg whites until they form stiff peaks, and fold into the

mixture. Pour into the pastry case and bake on Medium/360W for 10 minutes.

Combination cooking Bake the filled pastry case at 350°F/180°C on Medium/360W for 8 minutes.

Paris Brest

This is suitable for combination cooking only. Choux pastry is not the greatest of successes in the microwave but it is possible to get a reasonable result on a low microwave setting and a high oven temperature.

Serves 4
¼ pint (150 ml) water
2 oz (50 g) unsalted butter
3½ oz (90 g) wholemeal flour
1 free-range egg (size 2)

1. Line the microwave shelf or turntable with lightly oiled paper. Have ready a piping bag fitted with a 2 inch (1.75 cm) plain nozzle.
2. Place the water and butter in a jug or basin and melt on High/600W for 2.30 minutes. Transfer to a saucepan (a jug or basin is not really suitable for beating the pastry).
3. Sift the flour twice and pour into the butter and water. Beat vigorously with a wooden spoon until the mixture comes away from the sides of the pan in a clean shiny ball.
4. Lightly beat the egg and add half at a time, beating well between additions to make a stiff paste.
5. Place in a piping bag and pipe into a circle about 7 inches(/17.5 cm) in diameter on the paper.
6. Bake for 9 minutes at 425°F/218°C and power Lowest/90W, then lower the heat to 350°F/180°C and continue on power Lowest/90W for a further 5 minutes.
7. Remove from oven and leave until cold on a wire cooling tray.
8. Halve horizontally and fill with fresh fruit such as strawberries and raspberries, and Greek yoghurt.

Luxury Prune Flan

Serves 6-8

Pastry
4 oz (100 g) wholemeal flour
2 oz (50 g) soft vegetable margarine
2 drops lemon oil

Filling
12 oz (325 g) prunes
1 free-range egg white
2 oz (50 g) fructose
2 oz (50 g) ground almonds
2 oz (50 g) wholemeal flour

1. Soak the prunes overnight or place in a dish with a lid, with enough water to cover, and cook on High/600W for 5 minutes, stirring twice.
2. Lightly oil a 7 inch (17.5 cm) flan dish or other suitable serving dish.
3. Sift the flour into a mixing bowl and rub in the fat until the mixture resembles breadcrumbs in consistency.
4. Stir in enough cold water, mixed with the lemon oil, to make a soft dough. Roll out on a lightly floured surface and bake blind in the prepared dish.
5. Stone the prunes and arrange them in circles in the base of the pastry case.
6. Whisk the egg white until it is nearly stiff then add the fructose and continue whisking.
7. Fold in the almonds and the sieved flour and pour over the prunes, allowing the mixture to run evenly over the top.
8. Bake on High/600W for 4 minutes, then allow to stand for 5 minutes. Return to the oven again on High/600W for a further 2 minutes to finish off, if it is still a little sticky in the middle. Pat the top with absorbent kitchen paper if necessary.

Combination cooking Bake the filled tart at 400°F/200°C on Medium/360W for 5 minutes.

Fresh Apricot Cheesecake

Serves 8
1 lb (450 g) fresh apricots
6 oz (175 g) digestive biscuits
2 oz (50 g) soft vegetable margarine
2 free-range eggs (size 2) separated
3 oz (75 g) clear honey
½ lemon, grated rind of
8 oz (225 g) low-fat curd cheese
2 oz (50 g) ground almonds

1. Halve and stone the apricots, place in a dish with a lid and add enough water to almost cover them. Put the lid on and cook on High/600W for 8 minutes, stirring three times.
2. When cooked put under cold water to stop the cooking.

3. Crush the biscuits into crumbs.
4. Place the margarine in a basin or jug and melt on High/600W for 30 seconds. Stir into the crumbs and press into the base of a 7 inch (17.5 cm) flan dish or other suitable serving dish, or a microwave dish with a loose bottom.
5. Whisk the egg whites until they form stiff peaks.
6. Beat together the yolks and the honey until thick and pale in colour.
7. Beat the cheese, almonds and the lemon rind into the egg and honey, then fold in the egg white.
8. Place the apricot halves on top of the biscuit base. Pour the topping over and then bake on High/600W for 6 minutes. Remove from the oven and cool on a wire tray.

Combination cooking Bake at 350°F/180°C on Medium/360W for 5 minutes, followed by a further 2 minutes on conventional heat only.

Prune Pudding

Serves 8
4 oz (100 g) soft vegetable margarine
3 oz (75 g) clear honey
2-free range eggs, lightly beaten
2 tbsp skimmed milk
5 oz (150 g) wholemeal flour
½ tsp ground cinnamon
1 tsp baking powder
4 oz (100 g) stoned cooked or soaked prunes
2-3 tsp molasses

1. Line the base of an 8 inch (20 cm) cake dish.
2. Cream together the margarine and honey until light and fluffy in consistency.
3. Lightly beat in the eggs and milk.
4. Sift the flour, cinnamon and baking powder and fold into the mixture.
5. Place the prunes in the dish and spoon the cake mixture over them. Drizzle the molasses over the top in an attractive pattern.
6. Bake on High/600W for 5 minutes.

Combination cooking Bake at 350°F/180°C on Medium/360W for 6 minutes.

Peach and Apple Pie

Serves 8

Filling
2 lb (900 g) cooking apples
½ lemon, juice of
6 oz (175 g) dried peaches
2 oz (50 g) mixed dried fruit
½ tsp each ground cinnamon, ginger and cloves
3 tbsp no-added-sugar marmalade

Pastry
14 oz (400 g) wholemeal flour
1 tsp baking powder
4 oz (100 g) ground almonds
6 oz (175 g) soft vegetable margarine
cold water to mix

1. Peel, core and slice the apples into quite thick chunks and toss in the
lemon juice. Place in a dish with a lid and add about ½ inch (1 cm) water.
Cook, covered, on High/600W for about 4 minutes, stirring to ensure
even cooking.
2. Cook the dried peaches on High/600W in shallow water, stirring
twice, for about 5 minutes. Drain, reserving 2-3 tbsp of the juice for the
pie filling.
3. Sift the flour into a mixing bowl with the baking powder and stir in the
almonds.
4. Rub in the fat until the mixture resembles breadcrumbs in consistency,
then add enough water to make a soft dough. Divide into two pieces, roll
out on a floured surface, and line a 9 inch (22.5 cm) dish with half the
pastry. Spread the base with 2 tbsp of the marmalade, reserving enough to
glaze the lid.
5. Stir together the cooked apples and peaches and the dried fruit, spices
and the reserved peach juice. Place in the pie base. Roll out a lid from the
remaining pastry, place in position and bake on Medium/360W for 3
minutes, followed by 2 minutes on High/600W.
6. Remove from the oven and glaze the top with the remaining
marmalade. Serve hot, warm or cold.

Combination cooking Bake at 350°F/180°C on Medium/360W for 5
minutes followed by a further 3 minutes on conventional heat only.

Biscuits, Cookies, Scones' and Bars

THE DIFFERENCE between biscuits and cookies is that the former are British and crispy, usually because they are higher in fat and sugar, and the latter are American, larger, softer and chewier.

If you find some of your biscuits are overcooked and tough while others remain uncooked, or come out perfectly cooked, then hot spots will be to blame. Identify the spots and try not to place items in those positions.

As with conventional cooking, biscuits will need to be taken from the oven and left on a cooling tray to crisp. However, if you find the biscuits are still too chewy you can return them to the oven for a further 30 seconds, which should crisp them up. Err on the side of undercooking because overcooked biscuits will be hard and inedible.

Gingerbread People

Makes 16
8 oz (225 g) wholemeal flour
1 tsp baking powder
1 tsp ground ginger
½ tsp mixed spice
1½ oz (40 g) soft vegetable margarine
2 oz (50 g) molasses sugar
2 tbsp black treacle
4 tbsp boiling water
currants to decorate

1. Sift the flour into a mixing bowl together with the baking powder and spices.
2. Place the fat, sugar and treacle in a jug or basin and heat to dissolve on High/600W for 1.30 minutes.
3. Stir the treacle mixture into the flour, and if necessary add enough of the water to make a soft workable dough. Knead very lightly to enable the dough to be rolled out on a lightly floured board, then cut out the gingerbread people.
4. Place them on a lightly oiled microwave tray and position currants to make eyes, buttons or other features.
5. Cook in two batches of 8, on High/600W for 3 minutes.
6. Cool on a wire cooling tray, and then peel off the paper.
7. If liked, glaze while hot by brushing with a little clear honey.

Combination cooking   Bake at 375°F/190°C on Medium/360W for 4 minutes.

Carob or Chocolate Shortbread

Makes 8 slices
5 oz (150 g) wholemeal flour
1 oz (25 g) brown rice flour
2 oz (50 g) fructose
4 oz (100 g) unsalted butter
2 tbsp chocolate spread or carob alternative

1. Line a microwave tray.
2. Sift the flour into a mixing bowl and stir in the rice flour and fructose. Rub in the fat until the mixture is slightly sticky and then blend in the carob or chocolate spread using a large fork.
3. Knead lightly and roll out into a 6 inch (15 cm) circle on the paper-lined tray. Pinch up the edges and prick thoroughly. Slice through into 8 pieces.
4. Bake on Medium/360W for 5 minutes. Remove from the oven and tidy the edges if the mixture has spread a lot.
5. Lift off the paper, cut through again then allow to become cold on a wire cooling tray.

Combination cooking Bake at 325°F/160°C on Medium/360W for 5 minutes.

Carob Chip Cookies

Makes 14
2 oz (50 g) fructose
2 oz (50 g) soft vegetable margarine
2 drops natural vanilla essence
1 free-range egg, lightly beaten
4 oz (100 g) wholemeal flour
4½ oz (125 g) carob chips

1. Line a microwave tray.
2. Cream the fructose and margarine until pale and fluffy. Beat in the vanilla essence.
3. Beat in the egg, then fold in the sifted flour and finally the carob chips.
4. Place teaspoonfuls of the mixture on the tray and bake on High/600W for 2 minutes. Remove from the oven and cool slightly before peeling off the paper and cooling on a wire tray.

Combination cooking Bake at 375°F/190°C on Medium/360W for 4.30 minutes.

Light Ginger Biscuits

Makes 24
3 oz (75 g) wholemeal flour
1 tsp baking powder
3 tsp ground ginger
2 oz (50 g) medium oatmeal
2 oz (50 g) clear honey
2 oz (50 g) soft vegetable margarine

1. Line a microwave tray.
2. Sift the flour and baking powder and ginger into a mixing bowl and stir in the oatmeal.
3. Melt the honey and margarine in a basin or jug on High/600W for 1.30 minutes.
4. Mix all the ingredients well together and place heaped teaspoonfuls on the tray. Bake in two batches on High/600W for 1.30 minutes.
5. Remove and peel off the paper, then cool on a wire cooling tray.

Combination cooking Bake at 375°F/190°C on Medium/360W for 2 minutes.

Langues de Chat

Makes 30
2 oz (50 g) soft vegetable margarine
2 oz (50 g) light muscovado sugar
2 free-range egg yolks
1 drop natural vanilla essence
2 oz (50 g) wholemeal flour

1. Line a microwave tray.
2. Beat together all the ingredients until pale and creamy.
3. Place in a piping bag fitted with a ¼ inch (0.75 cm) plain nozzle and pipe 2½ inch (6 cm) long biscuits on to the tray.
4. Bake in two batches on High/600W for 2.30 minutes. Remove from the oven and peel off the paper then allow to cool on a wire tray.

Combination cooking Bake at 350°F/180°C on Medium/360W for 2 minutes.

Microwave Macaroons

Makes 18
2 sheets rice paper
2 free-range egg whites
3½ oz (85 g) ground almonds
1 oz (25 g) light muscovado sugar
1 tbsp cornflour
2 drops almond essence
flaked almonds to decorate (optional)

1. Line a microwave tray and place on top two sheets of rice paper side by side. Have ready a piping bag fitted with a plain ½ inch (1.75 cm) nozzle.
2. Whisk the egg whites until they form stiff peaks then fold in the remaining ingredients and place in the piping bag.
3. Pipe walnut-sized macaroons on to the paper, spacing them out well. Top each with a sliver of almond. You may need to bake them in two or three batches.
4. Bake on High/600W for 2 minutes for a crispier result, or on Medium/360W for 2.30 minutes for a softer result.
5. Remove from the oven and cool on a wire cooling tray. When cold trim the rice paper.

Combination cooking Bake at 300°F/150°C on Medium/360W for 3 minutes.

Date and Fig Bars

Makes 8 or 16
4 oz (100 g) cooking dates, chopped
4 oz (100 g) dried figs, chopped
¼ pint (150 ml) water
4 oz (100 g) soft vegetable margarine
3 oz (75 g) clear honey
12 oz (325 g) rolled oats

1. Line the base of a 2½ pint (1.25 litre) terrine measuring 9 × 4 inches (22.5 × 10 cm), and lightly oil.
2. Place the dates and figs in a dish with a lid and add the water. Cover and cook on High/600W for 5 minutes, stirring several times to ensure even cooking of the purée. Mash or liquidize.
3. Place the margarine and honey in a jug or basin and melt together on High/600W for 1.30 minutes.
4. Remove and stir in the oats. Place half the oat mixture in the base and press down firmly. Top with the purée, then cover with the other half of the oats and press down lightly.

5. Bake on High/600W for 5 minutes. Remove from the oven and grill the top to brown, if liked.
6. Cut into 8 bars, and halve the 8 again if you wish, but leave in the dish until completely cold. Then re-cut and turn out, peeling the paper off the base.

Combination cooking Bake at 350°F/180°C on Medium/360W for 8 minutes. Cut and cool as above.

Almond Slice

Cuts into 6-8 pieces
4 oz (100 g) soft vegetable margarine
3 oz (75 g) clear honey
1 free-range egg, lightly beaten
3 oz (75 g) ground almonds
2 oz (50 g) wholemeal flour
1 oz (25 g) brown rice flour or wholemeal semolina
2 oz (50 g) toasted flaked almonds
egg white to glaze

1. Line the base of a shallow baking dish or 1¼ pint (0.75 litre) terrine.
2. Cream together the margarine and honey until light and fluffy and beat in the egg.
3. Fold in the almonds, sifted flour and the brown rice flour or semolina, then spread in the prepared dish.
4. Sprinkle the toasted almonds on top and bake on High/600W for 4 minutes. Remove from the oven and glaze with a little egg white while still hot.
5. Stand for 5 minutes in the dish, remove and peel off the paper, then allow to become cold on a wire cooling tray, and slice.

Combination cooking Glaze and bake at 350°F/180°C on Medium/360W for 7 minutes.

Brownies

Makes 9
4 oz (100 g) soft vegetable margarine
4 oz (100 g) light muscovado sugar
2 free-range eggs
2 oz (50 g) wholemeal flour
1 tsp baking powder
1 oz (25 g) cocoa or carob powder
3 oz (75 g) walnuts, chopped

9 walnut halves for decoration
a little jam or honey

1. Line the base of a square 9 inch (22.5 cm) dish with lightly oiled greaseproof paper, for traditional square brownies, but if you do not have a square microwave dish use a terrine or cake dish and cut slices.
2. Cream together the margarine and sugar until light and fluffy in texture.
3. Lightly beat the eggs and add to the mixture, one at a time, adding a little flour between eggs if the mixture shows signs of curdling.
4. Sift the flour, baking powder and cocoa together and fold into the mixture together with the walnuts.
5. Spoon into the prepared dish and smooth the top. Bake for 4 minutes on High/600W.
6. Leave to stand and cool before removing from the dish, peeling off the paper and cutting into 9 squares, or slices. Place a walnut half on the top of each square, securing it in place with a blob of jam or honey.

Combination cooking Bake at 350°F /180°C on Medium/360W for 5 minutes.

Coconut Cookies

Makes 10
2 oz (50 g) wholemeal flour
1½ oz (40 g) soft vegetable margarine
2 oz (50 g) light muscovado sugar
1 oz (25 g) desiccated coconut
1 free-range egg (size 4)

1. Line a microwave tray.
2. Sift the flour into a mixing bowl and rub in the fat until the mixture resembles breadcrumbs in consistency.
3. Stir in the sugar and coconut and bind with the egg to make a soft dough.
4. Roll balls about the size of a walnut and then place on the prepared tray and press down with a fork.
5. Bake on Medium/360W for 3.30 minutes. Remove from the oven, peel off the paper and cool on a wire cooling tray.

Combination cooking Bake at 350°F/180°C on High/600W for 2.30 minutes.

Oat Cookies

Makes 10
2 oz (50 g) clear honey
2 oz (50 g) soft vegetable margarine
2 oz (50 g) wholemeal flour
2 oz (50 g) rolled oats

1. Line a microwave tray.
2. Place the honey and margarine in a jug or basin and melt on High/600W for 1.30 minutes. Remove and stir well.
3. Sift the flour into a mixing bowl and stir in the oats.
4. Pour on the honey mixture and mix well. Place spoonfuls on the prepared tray and press down with a fork to flatten into cookie shapes.
5. Bake for 3 minutes on High/600W.
6. Remove and peel off the paper then cool on a wire cooling tray.

Combination cooking Bake at 375°F/190°C on Medium/360W for 3.30 minutes.

Almond Butter Biscuits

Makes 20
2 oz (50 g) wholemeal flour
2 oz (50 g) brown rice flour
3 oz (75 g) almond butter
1 free-range egg
1 tbsp sunflower oil
1 tbsp clear honey
2 tbsp boiling water

1. Line a microwave tray.
2. Sift the flour into a mixing bowl and stir in the rice flour.
3. Beat together the almond butter, egg, oil, honey and water.
4. Stir the beaten ingredients into the flour mixture, then work to produce a pliable dough. Roll out and cut out 2 inch (5cm) biscuits.
5. Place the biscuits on the prepared tray and bake in two batches of 10 for 2 minutes.
6. Remove from the oven and peel off the paper, then cool on a wire cooling tray.

Combination cooking Bake at 350°F/180°C on Medium/360W for 2.30 minutes.

Walnut Biscuits

Makes 10
2 oz (50 g) soft vegetable margarine
2 oz (50 g) light muscovado sugar
1 oz (25 g) walnuts, chopped
2 tbsp skimmed milk
3 oz (75 g) wholemeal flour
no-added-sugar jam, or a little clear honey
a few more finely chopped nuts

1. Line a microwave tray.
2. Cream together the margarine and sugar, then beat in the nuts and skimmed milk.
3. Sift the flour and fold into the mixture.
4. Take walnut-sized balls and space them on the prepared tray, then press down lightly with a fork to make flat biscuits.
5. Bake for 3.30 minutes. Remove from the oven and cool on a wire tray.
6. If liked, brush the tops with a little no-added-sugar jam or clear honey and sprinkle on some finely chopped walnuts.

Combination cooking Bake at 375°F/190°C on High/600W for 2 minutes.

Malted Carob Slice

Serves 8
4 oz (100 g) soft vegetable margarine
1 oz (25 g) light muscovado sugar
2 tbsp malt extract
8 oz (225 g) rolled oats
4 oz (100 g) plain carob
2 tbsp black decaffeinated coffee

1. Line the base of a shallow 7 inch (17.5 cm) dish and lightly oil.
2. Place the margarine, sugar and malt extract in a jug or basin and melt in the oven on High/600W for 1.30 minutes. Remove and stir well to combine.
3. Stir the margarine mixture into the oats and then press lightly into the prepared dish.
4. Bake on High/600W for 4 minutes. Remove the dish and cut through into 8 slices, but do not remove from the dish until completely cold when the slices will have to be re-cut.
5. When the cold slices are cut, melt the carob by placing in a jug or basin with the coffee and heating on High/600W for 1.30 minutes. Stir well.

6. Coat the base of the slices with the carob and leave upside down on a wire cooling tray to set – this can be speeded by placing in the fridge/freezer.

Combination cooking Bake at 375°F/190°C on High/600W for 3.30 minutes.

Carob Cookies

Makes 16
3 oz (75 g) soft vegetable margarine
3 oz (75 g) dark muscovado sugar
1½ oz (40 g) sunflower seeds
2 oz (50 g) carob chips or drops
4 oz (100 g) wholemeal flour
1 tbsp skimmed milk

1. Line a microwave tray.
2. Cream together the fat and sugar until pale in colour and of a soft dropping consistency.
3. Stir in the sunflower seeds and carob chips.
4. Sift the flour and fold into the mixture. Moisten, if necessary, with the milk.
5. Place heaped teaspoonfuls on the paper and bake on Medium/360W for 2.30 minutes.
6. Remove from the oven and stand for 5 minutes on the paper before peeling it off and leaving the cookies to become cold on a wire cooling tray.

Combination cooking Bake at 375°F/190°C on Medium/360W for 2 minutes.

Flapjack

Makes 8
3 oz (75 g) Demerara sugar
4 oz (100 g) soft vegetable margarine
2 oz (50 g) golden syrup
8 oz (225 g) rolled oats

1. Lightly oil an 8 inch (20 cm) dish.
2. Place the sugar, margarine and golden syrup in a jug and melt together on High/600W for 1.30 minutes.
3. Stir the oats into the melted mixture and press into the dish.
4. Cook on High/600W for 4 minutes.

5. Remove from the oven and cut through with a knife, but leave in the dish until completely cold. Cut through again and remove.

Combination cooking Bake at 350°F/180°C on High/600W for 3.30 minutes.

Sesame Flapjacks

Sesame seeds have a delicious taste and add some crunch to the flapjacks. Make the basic mixture as above, but when adding the oats add 3 oz (75 g) sesame seeds that have been lightly browned on the microwave griddle or browning dish, or under the grill or in a hot pan without added fat.

Mincemeat Flapjacks

Again, use the basic flapjack mixture, but stir in 3 oz (75 g) mincemeat to the melted ingredients.

Date Slice

Makes 8 or 16
5 oz (150 g) cooking dates, chopped
2 tbsp water
2 tbsp concentrated apple juice
4 oz (100 g) wholemeal flour
3 oz (75 g) soft vegetable margarine
2 oz (50 g) rolled oats
2 oz (50 g) dark muscovado sugar

1. Lightly oil a 9 × 4 inch (22.5 × 10 cm) terrine or a 6 inch (15 cm) cake dish.
2. Place the dates in a dish with a lid together with the water and apple juice. Cover and cook on High/600W for 4 minutes, stirring once. Remove and mash or liquidize to a purée.
3. Sift the flour into a mixing bowl and rub in the fat until the mixture resembles breadcrumbs in consistency. Stir in the oats and sugar and work a little to make it a bit sticky.
4. Lightly press half into the base of the dish and cover with the date mixture. Top with the rest of the oats and press down lightly.
5. Bake on High/600W for 4 minutes. Remove from the oven and cut across into 8 bars, but leave until completely cold before cutting through again and removing from the dish.
6. Cut each slice into half, if liked.

Combination cooking Bake at 375°F/190°C on High/600W for 3.30 minutes.

Sultana Scones

Makes 8
8 oz (225 g) wholemeal flour
1 tsp baking powder
2 oz (50 g) soft vegetable margarine
2 oz (50 g) sultanas
2 oz (50 g) light muscovado sugar (optional)
¼ pint (150 ml) skimmed milk

1. Line a microwave tray and have ready a 1½ inch (3.75 cm) scone cutter.
2. Sift the flour into a mixing bowl with the baking powder.
3. Rub in the fat until the mixture resembles breadcrumbs in consistency.
4. Stir in the sugar (if liked) and sultanas, then bind with the milk to make a soft dough.
5. Knead very lightly to make the dough pliable enough to roll out. Then cut out the scones and place on the tray. Dust the tops with a little flour through a sieve.
6. Bake on High/600W for 3 minutes. Peel off the paper and turn the scones upside down. Return to the oven for a further 30 seconds. Remove and cool on a wire cooling tray.

Combination cooking Glaze and bake at 375°F/190°C on High/600W for 2.30 minutes.

Note If you are not keen on the floured look, you can brush the tops with clear honey instead of flour, or glaze with egg wash and pop under a hot grill for a minute to brown the tops. The sugar is optional. If you do not have a sweet tooth, or if you are trying to give up sugar, omit and sweeten the scones by adding a teaspoonful of mixed spice.

Walnut and Honey Cookies

Makes 24
4 oz (100 g) soft vegetable margarine
2 oz (50 g) light muscovado sugar
2 oz (50 g) walnut pieces, finely chopped
2 oz (50 g) clear honey
6 oz (175 g) wholemeal flour

1. Line a microwave tray.
2. Cream together the margarine and sugar until light and fluffy.
3. Add the nuts and honey.
4. Sift the flour and fold into the mixture.
5. Place large walnut-sized balls of the biscuit mixture well spaced on the

paper. Press lightly with a fork to flatten and indent the top with a pattern.

5. Bake about 7-8 biscuits at a time on Medium/360W for 3-3.30 minutes. Remove from the oven and when slightly cool peel off the paper and leave to become completely cold on a wire cooling tray.

Combination cooking Bake at 350°F/180°C on High/600W for 2.30 minutes.

Oatmeal and Sultana Slice

Makes 8 slices
2 oz (50 g) soft vegetable margarine
5 oz (150 g) medium or fine oatmeal
3 oz (75 g) raisins
2 oz (50 g) Demerara sugar
2 oz (50 g) wholemeal flour, sieved
⅛ pint (75 ml) boiling water

1. Have ready a lightly oiled 6 inch (15 cm) dish.
2. Place the margarine in a jug and melt on High/600W for 60 seconds.
3. Place the oatmeal and other dry ingredients in a mixing bowl and stir in the melted margarine and the water to make a soft dough.
4. Press the dough lightly into the dish and bake on Medium/360W for 6 minutes.
5. Remove from the oven and while hot cut through to mark the 8 slices. When completely cold re-cut and remove.

Combination cooking Bake at 350°F/180°C on Medium/360W for 4.30 minutes.

Florentines

Makes 20
2 oz (50 g) soft vegetable margarine
3 oz (75 g) light muscovado sugar
1½ oz (40 g) flaked almonds, lightly toasted (this is the secret ingredient!)
1 oz (25 g) walnut pieces, finely chopped
1 oz (25 g) glacé cherries, chopped
1½ oz (40g) sultanas
1 oz (25 g) mixed peel
1 oz (25 g) mixed dried fruit
2 oz (50 g) plain dark chocolate or carob

1. Line a microwave tray and dust with sifted flour.
2. Place the margarine and sugar in a basin and melt on High/600W for 2.30 minutes, stirring once or twice.
3. Mix the sugar and margarine well and stir in the rest of the ingredients (except the chocolate) – the fat might separate out a bit, but this doesn't matter because it means you get less in the end-product.
4. Place small blobs of the mixture, well spaced, on the paper. You can bake about 9 at a time. Cook on High/600W for 2.30 minutes.
5. Remove from the oven and place the paper on a wire cooling tray. Tidy the edges of the florentines and put in the fridge to set. Bake the rest.
6. When they are all cold melt the chocolate by breaking up into squares and placing in a bowl in the microwave. Heat on High/600W for 60 seconds. Remove and stir the chocolate then spread it over the base of the florentines. Leave them upside-down until almost set then either put squiggles with a fork on the base, or invert them and have the indented pattern of the cooling tray on the base.

Chocolate Digestives

Makes 10
2 oz (50 g) self-raising wholemeal flour
1 oz (25 g) medium or fine oatmeal
2 oz (50 g) soft vegetable margarine
1 oz (25 g) dark muscovado sugar
skimmed milk to mix
2 oz (50 g) plain chocolate or carob
2 tbsp water
¼ oz (6 g) unsalted butter

1. Line a microwave tray.
2. Sift the flour into a mixing bowl and stir in the oatmeal.
3. Rub in the fat until the mixture resembles breadcrumbs in consistency.
4. Stir in the sugar and then bind with a little milk to make a soft biscuit dough.
5. Roll out on a lightly floured surface and cut out 3 inch (7.5 cm) biscuit rounds. Place them on the tray and bake on High/600W for 3.30 minutes.
6. Remove and place on a wire cooling tray.
7. When cold, place the chocolate and water in a dish and melt on High/600W for 2 minutes. Remove from the oven and stir in the butter. Spread over the top of the biscuits and leave until almost set, then squiggle patterns on the top with a fork or the point of a knife.

Combination cooking Bake at 350°F/180°C on Medium/360W for 4 minutes.

Currant Biscuits

Makes 12
2 oz (50 g) soft vegetable margarine
2 oz (50 g) fructose
1 free-range egg yolk
1 oz (25 g) currants
2 oz (50 g) wholemeal flour

1. Line a microwave tray and have ready a 2 inch (5 cm) fancy-edged biscuit cutter.
2. Cream together the margarine, fructose and egg yolk.
3. Stir in the currants, then fold in the sifted flour.
4. Roll out on a lightly floured board and cut out the biscuits.
5. Place on the tray and bake on High/600W for 2.30 minutes.
6. Remove from the oven and, if liked, brush the tops with egg white and put under the grill to brown for 1.30 minutes.

Combination cooking Glaze with egg white and bake at 375°F/190°C on Medium/360W for 4 minutes.

Viennese Fingers

Makes 24 plain or 12 filled fingers
4 oz (100 g) soft vegetable margarine
1 oz (25 g) fructose
5 oz (150 g) wholemeal flour
2 oz (50 g) chocolate or carob (optional)
2 tbsp black decaffeinated coffee (optional)
no-added-sugar jam to sandwich (optional)

1. Line a microwave tray.
2. Cream together the margarine, fructose and flour and place in a piping bag with a plain ½ inch (1.25 cm) nozzle.
3. Pipe 24 finger biscuits on to the tray and bake on High/600W for 2.30 minutes.
4. Remove from the oven and when cool enough to handle peel off the paper and place on a wire cooling tray.
5. If you are going to dip the ends of the fingers in chocolate or carob, place the broken-up bar in a dish together with the coffee and heat on High/600W for 60 seconds to melt. Remove and stir.
6. If liked, sandwich the biscuits together in pairs using a little jam, then dip each, or one, end into the chocolate/carob.

Combination cooking Bake at 350°F/180°C on High/600W for 2 minutes.

Cheese Scones

Makes 8
8 oz (225 g) wholemeal flour
pinch sea salt
1 tsp mustard powder
2 oz (50 g) soft vegetable margarine
2 oz (50 g) mature Cheddar cheese, grated
1 oz (25 g) Gruyère cheese, grated
¼ pint (150 ml) skimmed milk

1. Line a microwave tray and have ready a 2½ inch (7.5 cm) scone cutter.
2. Sift the flour into a mixing bowl together with the salt and mustard powder.
3. Rub in the fat until the mixture resembles breadcrumbs in consistency, then stir in the cheese.
4. Mix in the milk to make a soft dough. Lightly knead until you can roll out the dough to a thickness of about 1 inch (2.5 cm), then cut out the scones.
5. Either dust the tops with a little sifted wholemeal flour or brush with an egg or milk glaze. Place on the tray and bake on High/600W for 4.30 minutes. Re-glaze and brown under the grill, if liked.

Combination cooking Glaze and bake at 400°F/200°C on High/600W for 3.30 minutes.

Flapjack (page 76) and Almond Slice (page 72)

SAVOURY PIES,
FLANS AND PASTRIES

Viennese Fingers (page 81), Chocolate Digestives (page 80) and Microwave Macaroons (page 71)

WHOLEMEAL FLOUR gives a new dimension to microbaked pastry because it adds colour and a delicious nutty flavour. Many recipes use baked blind pastry cases but microbaking can also be excellent for pies and pastries other than flans. Combination ovens are a fantastic boon for pastry-making in the microwave because the conventional heat helps bake a crisper and drier pastry while the microwaves speed the process.

Yeasted pastry is also a great success in both microwave and combination oven. It is very easy to make and gives a much lighter finish than standard shortcrust or puff pastry, and it has the benefit of being lower in fat than both. Because microwave proving and rising is very speedy, microbaking allows yeasted pastry to appear more frequently on the menu. It freezes well, too.

For the best results with all pastries remember not to cover the dish (unless baking blind) while it is cooking or you will trap steam and make it soggy. If you roll the pastry too thick it may also go soggy. The idea is to keep pastry as crisp and dry as possible.

To bake blind, proceed as follows:
1. Lightly oil the dish and line with the pastry.
2. Prick the pastry and place a layer of greaseproof, baking or silicone baking paper on top of the pastry.
3. Place a plate or some baking beans on top of the paper to weigh the pastry down.
4. Bake on High/600W for 2 minutes.
5. Remove the plate/beans and paper and bake for another 30 seconds or, if the case is to be used without further cooking, for another 1.30 minutes.

Combination cooking Proceed as for microbaking then cook at 400°F/200°C on High/600W for 2 minutes. Remove the plate/beans and paper and cook for a further 60 seconds.

Koubillac

This is a traditional Russian fish pie. It is very tasty and makes a popular family meal or can be cut into slices and served warm or cold at parties.

Serves 4 as a main course, 10 for a buffet

Filling
4 oz (100 g) brown rice
2 free-range eggs, hardboiled
12 oz (325 g) fresh salmon
freshly ground black pepper
2 tbsp chopped fresh parsley, or 1 tbsp dried

Yeasted pastry
8 oz (225 g) wholemeal flour
2 oz (50 g) unsalted butter
⅛ pint (75 ml) lukewarm water
½ oz (12 g) fresh yeast
1 free-range egg
a little egg wash or skimmed milk to glaze
a little parsley for decoration

1. First prepare the filling ingredients.
2. Wash the rice and cover with twice the volume of boiling water in a deep bowl. Cover and cook on High/600W for 20 minutes, topping up if necessary.
3. Place the salmon in a dish with a lid, together with enough vegetable stock to almost cover, and cook on Medium/360W for 8 minutes then flake from the skin and bone.
4. Line a microwave tray.
5. Sift the flour into a mixing bowl and rub in the fat until the mixture resembles breadcrumbs in consistency.
6. Measure the water into a jug, crumble in the yeast and stir to make a paste.
7. Lightly beat the egg, then mix the yeast and egg into the flour to make a soft dough.
8. Turn the dough on to a lightly floured board and knead until it is possible to roll out.
9. Roll the dough into a large rectangle about 20 × 14 inches (50 × 30 cm). Now put the pastry on to the lined tray. Place a layer of rice on one half of the base (the other half is to be folded over to make a square parcel), topped by half the parsley and half the sliced hardboiled egg, followed by the flaked salmon, the rest of the parsley and egg and then the remainder of the rice. Season the layers with pepper to taste.
10. Fold over the other half of the pastry and seal the edges with egg wash. Press down and pinch into place to make an attractive edge.
11. Prove in the oven on High/600W for 15 seconds, then leave to stand for 10 minutes.
12. Cook on High/600W for 5 minutes. Leave to rest for 5 minutes and then cook for a further 4 minutes.
13. Glaze and brown under the grill, if liked. Decorate with the parsley before serving.

Combination cooking When complete, glaze and bake at 375°F/190°C on High/600W for 7 minutes, turning once or twice.

Anchovy Pizza

Makes 2 pizzas of 7 inches (17.5 cm)

Dough
8 oz (225 g) wholemeal flour
pinch sea salt (optional)
½ oz (12 g) fresh yeast
¼ pint (150 ml) lukewarm water

Topping
2 tbsp tomato purée
2 tsp dried or 2 tbsp fresh mixed chopped herbs
1 large onion, diced
2 carrots, diced
7 oz (200 g) canned tomatoes, crushed
2 oz (50 g) can anchovies
10-12 green olives
3½ oz (90 g) mozarella cheese

1. Lightly oil two 7 inch (17.5 cm) pizza dishes or plates.
2. Sift the flour into a mixing bowl and stir in the salt, if using.
3. Crumble the yeast into the water and mix to a paste, then pour into the flour and mix well to make a soft dough.
4. Knead the dough for 3 minutes, then prove on High/600W for 15 seconds and rest for 10 minutes.
5. Divide into two. Roll out the pieces of dough and place them on the prepared dishes.
6. Spread with the tomato purée and sprinkle with the herbs, then leave to rest while you prepare the topping.
7. Place the onion, carrots and tomatoes in a dish with a lid and sweat them on High/600W for 8 minutes, stirring twice.
8. Drain the anchovies and pat off excess oil using absorbent kitchen paper.
9. Top the purée with the tomato and vegetable mixture and arrange the anchovies and olives on top.
10. Slice the cheese very thinly and place on the top, then bake the pizzas for 10-12 minutes on Medium/360W. Place one on a shelf in the oven and one on the base and swap positions half-way through cooking, or bake them one after the other for 8 minutes each if you do not have this facility. Brown the tops under the grill, if liked.

Combination cooking Bake the pizzas separately for 8 minutes each at 400°F/200°C on Medium/360W, or if cooking both together for 12 minutes, swapping positions half-way through cooking.

Note You can use the ingredients to make one large pizza with the base rolled out to fit the lightly oiled tray of your oven. Increase cooking time for a single pizza by 1-1.30 minutes.

Sardine Pizza

Makes 2 pizzas of 7 inches (17.5 cm)

1 quantity of pizza dough (see Anchovy Pizza recipe above)
1 red pepper, diced
1 onion, diced
1 carrot, diced
2 large tomatoes, roughly chopped
pinch tarragon
4 large mushrooms, sliced
4 oz (100 g) can sardines in tomato sauce
1 dsp capers

1. Lightly oil the microwave tray(s) or two 7 inch (17.5 cm) dishes or plates, and make the dough as for Anchovy Pizza (page 86, steps 2-5).
2. To make the topping, place all the prepared vegetables (except the mushrooms) together with the tarragon in a dish with a lid and cook, covered, on High/600W for 10 minutes, stirring twice to ensure even cooking.
3. Spread the vegetable mixture over the pizza bases, then arrange the sardines and mushroom slices over the vegetables and scatter the capers on top.
4. Bake on High/600W for 4.30 minutes if cooking separately, or place one on a shelf and one on the floor of the oven and bake for 8 minutes, swapping positions half-way through cooking.

Combination cooking Bake at 400°F/200°C on High/600W for 4 minutes or, if cooking together, cook for 8 minutes, and swap positions half-way through.

Note You can use the ingredients to make one large pizza with the base rolled out to fit the lightly oiled tray of your oven. Increase cooking time for a single pizza by 1-1.30 minutes.

Vegetable and Beef Pie

Serves 6

Pastry
6 oz (175 g) wholemeal flour
3 oz (75 g) soft vegetable margarine

cold water to mix
egg wash to glaze

Filling
1 lb (450 g) lean stewing beef
1 tbsp wholemeal flour
freshly ground black pepper
pinch sea salt
2 large onions, diced
2 cloves garlic, crushed
1 green pepper, deseeded and diced
2 carrots, diced
1 parsnip, diced
1 vegetable bouillon cube
1 pint (600 ml) boiling water
1 tbsp HP or Whole Earth Kensington sauce
1 dsp tomato purée
1 tsp each dried basil and dill

1. Have ready a large 9 inch (22.5 cm) pie dish.
2. Dice the beef and trim off any excess fat. Toss in the flour and seasoning and cook on High/600W in a large covered dish for 10 minutes, stirring twice.
3. Add the prepared vegetables and continue to cook on High/600W for a further 15 minutes, stirring two or three times to ensure even cooking.
4. Add the boiling water to the stock cube and mix in the rest of the ingredients, then pour on to the meat and vegetables. Continue cooking on Medium/360W for 20 minutes, stirring two or three times.
5. While the pie filling is cooking make the pastry. Sift the flour into a mixing bowl. Rub in the fat until the mixture resembles breadcrumbs in consistency.
6. Mix with enough cold water to make a soft dough and roll out a lid for the pie. Also cut out a strip to fit around the edge of the dish.
7. Transfer the meat from the covered dish to the pie dish in which it is to be served (this can, of course, be the same dish).
8. Glaze the pastry strip with water and place in position around the edge of the dish, glaze again and affix the lid to it. Pierce a hole in the lid and then bake the pie on High/600W for 10 minutes. If liked, glaze the top with egg wash and brown under the grill.

Combination cooking Glaze with egg wash and bake the pie at 400°F/200°C on Medium/360W for 15 minutes. You can also pre-cook the filling in a combination oven heated to 325°F/160°C and High/600W allowing 10 minutes for each stage.

Nutmeat Rolls

Makes about 10

Pastry
5 oz (150 g) wholemeal flour
3 oz (75 g) soft vegetable margarine
cold water to mix
egg wash or skimmed milk to glaze

Nutmeat
1 onion, grated
1 carrot, grated
1 dsp mixed chopped fresh herbs
   such as sage, thyme, parsley, or
    1 tsp dried mixed herbs
4 oz (100 g) mixed ground nuts
4 oz (100 g) wholemeal breadcrumbs
1 free-range egg, lightly beaten
2 tbsp vegetable stock

1. Line a microwave shelf or tray with a layer of lightly oiled greaseproof paper.
2. Sift the flour into a mixing bowl and rub in the fat until the mixture resembles breadcrumbs in consistency.
3. Mix with enough cold water to make a soft dough and cover until required.
4. To make the filling simply mix all the remaining ingredients to a nutmeat paste.
5. Roll out the pastry on a lightly floured board into a long rectangle about 12 × 8 inches (30 × 20 cm).
6. With floured hands roll the nutmeat into a long sausage and place in strips across the width of the pastry rectangle ½ inch (1.75 cm) from the edge and at 3 inch (7.5 cm) intervals as you would do to make sausage rolls. Slice across.
7. Brush the edges of the pastry with egg wash and fold it over the nutmeat, sealing the edge by pinching it or knocking it up with the side of a knife.
8. Re-roll scraps of pastry and use up remaining filling.
9. Cut each strip into 3 and score the tops of the rolls diagonally. Bake on High/600W for 4-5 minutes.
10. Reglaze and brown under the grill after cooking, or when reheating the rolls to serve, if liked.

Combination cooking Glaze and bake at 400°F/200°C on Medium/360W for 6 minutes.

Liver Pâté en Croûte

Serves 8

Pastry
8 oz (225 g) wholemeal flour
3 oz (75 g) soft vegetable margarine
pinch sea salt (optional)
cold water to mix
egg wash to glaze

Pâté
8 oz (225 g) liver
1 onion, diced
1 clove garlic, crushed
¼ oz (6 g) unsalted butter
1 tbsp chopped parsley
freshly ground black pepper
1 tbsp tomato ketchup

1. Line a microwave tray.
2. Sift the flour into a mixing bowl, and add the salt if using. Rub in the fat until the mixture resembles breadcrumbs in consistency, and mix to a soft dough with a little cold water. Cover while you prepare the pâté.
3. Trim and dice the liver and place with the onion, garlic and butter in a dish. Cover and cook on High/600W for 5 minutes, stirring twice to ensure even cooking.
4. Remove from the dish and liquidize with the parsley, pepper and ketchup to make a fine or coarse pâté, as preferred.
5. Roll out the pastry to a rectangle about 12 × 9 inches (30 × 22.5 cm). Place the pâté in the centre of the pastry in a rectangle about 7 × 3 inches (17.5 × 8 cm).
6. Cut the pastry from the edge of the pâté out to the edge of the pastry in strips about 1½ inches (4 cm) wide. Brush the strips with egg wash and then fold them up over the centre to envelop the pâté.
7. Bake on High/600W for 7 minutes. Remove, then glaze and brown under the grill, if liked.

Combination cooking Glaze and bake at 400°F/200°C on Medium/360W for 6 minutes.

Fish Pasties

Makes 6

Yeasted pastry
10 oz (275 g) wholemeal flour

1 oz (25 g) soft vegetable margarine
¼ pint (150 ml) water
½ oz (12 g) fresh yeast
egg wash or skimmed milk to glaze

Filling
12 oz (325 g) smoked haddock
1 large onion
2 oz (50 g) mushrooms
⅛ pint (75 ml) white wine
freshly ground black pepper

1. Sift the flour into a mixing bowl and then rub in the fat until the mixture resembles breadcrumbs in consistency.
2. Measure the water into a jug and heat on High/600W for 15 seconds. Remove from the heat and crumble in the yeast. Mix into the flour and knead a little, then prove on High/600W for 15 seconds and leave, covered, to rest while preparing the filling.
3. Poach the fish in enough water to cover, in a dish with a lid, on High/600W for 5 minutes. Remove and run under cold water. When cool enough to handle flake the fish from the bone and skin, into a mixing bowl.
4. Dice the onion and place in a covered dish with the sliced mushrooms and the wine and poach on Medium/360W for 4 minutes. Drain and mix with the fish. Season.
5. Roll out the dough and cut into 12 fish shapes. When the filling is cold, place some down the middle of 6 of the shapes and glaze the edges. Place a second fish shape on top, then knock up the sides with a knife to seal.
6. Place the fish on the lined microwave shelf or turntable and bake on High/600W for 5 minutes.
7. Remove, brush with egg wash and lightly brown under the grill, if liked.

Combination cooking　Glaze and bake at 400°F/200°C on Medium/360W for 6 minutes.

Watercress Fish Pie

Serves 4

Filling
1 large leek, trimmed and sliced
1 large potato, diced
1 tbsp wholemeal flour
1 tbsp vegetable oil

½ pint (300 ml) vegetable stock
sea salt and freshly ground black pepper
1 bunch watercress
8 oz (225 g) white fish of choice, filleted, skinned and cubed

Pastry
5 oz (150 g) wholemeal flour
1 oz (25 g) medium oatmeal
2 oz (50 g) soft vegetable margarine
skimmed milk to mix
egg wash or skimmed milk to glaze

1. Place the leek and potato in a covered dish with some of the stock and
cook on High/600W for 5 minutes, stirring once.
2. Make a roux by stirring together the flour and oil in a jug and cooking
on High/600W for 30 seconds. Remove and stir. Repeat.
3. Gradually add the vegetable stock, cooking in the oven in the same
way and stirring between additions at 30 second intervals. Season to taste.
4. Place the sauce and the washed watercress in a food processor and
blend until smooth.
5. Put the potato and leek in the base of the pie dish with the cubed fish
and pour the sauce over.
6. Make the pastry by sifting the flour into a mixing bowl and stirring in
the oatmeal.
7. Rub in the fat until the mixture resembles breadcrumbs in consistency
and then carefully mix in enough milk to make a soft dough.
8. Roll out on a floured surface to make a rim and a lid for the pie. Fix in
position with a little egg wash and bake on High/600W for 7 minutes.
9. Remove from the oven and, if liked, glaze with more egg wash and
carefully brown under the grill.

Combination cooking Glaze and bake at 400°F/200°C on
Medium/360W for 10 minutes.

Steak and Kidney Pie

Serves 2

Filling
1 onion, diced
4 oz (100 g) mushrooms, sliced
4 oz (100 g) kidney
6 oz (175 g) lean stewing steak or beef
1 tbsp flour
sea salt and freshly ground black pepper
1 tsp readymade mustard
1 tbsp HP or Whole Earth Kensington sauce

Pastry
8 oz (225 g) wholemeal flour
3½ oz (90 g) soft vegetable margarine
cold water to mix
a little egg wash or skimmed milk to glaze

1. Place the onion and mushrooms in a dish with a lid and cook on
High/600W for 5 minutes, stirring twice.
2. Dice the steak and kidney and toss in seasoned flour, then cook on
Low/180W for 10 minutes, stirring from time to time. Add the brown
sauce and the mustard and continue cooking for another 5 minutes,
stirring twice. Stir in the vegetables, adjust seasoning, and leave on one
side.
3. Sift the flour into a mixing bowl. Rub in the fat until the mixture
resembles breadcrumbs in consistency and then add enough water to make
a soft dough. Roll out and line a 6 inch (15 cm) lightly oiled dish with the
pastry, leaving enough to make a lid and a rim for the pie, and bake blind
on High/600W for 2 minutes. (For details of baking blind, see page 000.)
4. Add the filling to the pie and make a rim around the edge of the dish
with pastry. Fix the lid to the rim and bake on Medium/360W for 10
minutes. Remove and glaze the top with egg wash or milk and carefully
brown under the grill.

Combination cooking Glaze and bake at 375°F/190°C on
Medium/360W for 10 minutes.

Countrybake Pie

Serves 4

Pastry
4 oz (100 g) wholemeal flour
2 oz (50 g) soft vegetable margarine
cold water to mix

Filling
1 parsnip
1 carrot
½ red pepper
1 onion
8 brussels sprouts
½ vegetable stock cube dissolved in ½ pint (300 ml) water
sea salt
freshly ground black pepper
1 tbsp HP or Whole Earth Kensington sauce
2 tsp arrowroot or cornflour

2 tbsp cold water
3 oz (75 g) cooked brown lentils
2 oz (50 g) grated mature Cheddar cheese

1. Sift the flour into a mixing bowl. Rub in the fat until the mixture resembles breadcrumbs in consistency. Add enough cold water to make a soft dough and roll out the pastry to fit the top of an 8 inch (20 cm) pie dish. Also cut a rim to go round the edge of the dish on to which the lid will be fixed.
2. Peel and slice the vegetables, but just trim the sprouts and cut a cross in their bases.
3. Place the vegetables in a dish with a lid and add the stock. Cover and cook on High/600W for about 10 minutes, stirring three times during the cooking. Season to taste. Add the brown sauce.
4. Mix the arrowroot with 2 tbsp water and stir into the vegetables to thicken the sauce. Stir in the lentils, and place the mixture in the base of the pie dish.
5. Fix the pastry rim in position and top with the lid. Cut a slit in the lid.
6. Bake on High/600W for 10 minutes, then sprinkle the cheese on top of the pie and finish off under the grill to brown.

Combination cooking Place the cheese on top and bake at 400°F/200°C on Medium/360W for 15 minutes.

Sweet Potato Pie

Serves 2-3

Yeasted pastry
10 oz (275 g) wholemeal flour
1½ oz (40 g) Gruyère cheese, grated
8 fl. oz (240 ml) water
½ oz (12 g) fresh yeast
a little egg wash or skimmed milk to glaze

Filling
4 shallots, peeled
1 leek, trimmed and sliced
1 small sweet potato (unpeeled), diced
¼ pint (150 ml) vegetable stock
1 tsp arrowroot or cornflour
1 tbsp cold water
7 oz (200 g) cooked chickpeas

1. Sift the flour into a mixing bowl. Stir in the cheese.
2. Place the water in a jug and heat on High/600W for 30 seconds.

Remove from heat and crumble in the yeast. Add to the flour and mix to a soft dough.

3. Roll out on a floured board. Line a 7 inch (17.5 cm) pie dish and cut out a lid.

4. Place the shallots, leek and potato in a dish with a lid, together with the stock, and cook on High/600W for 10 minutes, stirring about three times during cooking.

5. Thicken the stock the vegetables have cooked in by stirring in the arrowroot mixed with the cold water.

6. Stir in the chickpeas and then place the filling in the prepared dish. Cover with the pastry lid, sealing the edges of lid and pie base with a little egg wash or milk.

7. Prove on High/600W for 15 seconds and leave to rest for 10 minutes, then bake on Medium/360W for 12 minutes.

Combination cooking Glaze and bake at 400°F/200°C on Medium/360W for 10 minutes.

Lamb Samosas

This is a fiddly job, so you are 'allowed' to start out with a packet of readymade wholemeal pastry to make it a bit quicker and easier. (You can, of course, use packet pastry for any of the other recipes you choose.)

Makes 24
14 oz (400 g) pack wholemeal pastry, thawed
1 large onion, diced
8 oz (225 g) ground lamb
½ red pepper, diced
3 tomatoes, roughly chopped
2 tsp each white mustard seed and ground cumin
2 oz (50 g) frozen peas
a little egg wash to glaze

1. Line a microwave tray.

2. Place the onion and lamb in a dish with a lid, cover and cook on High/600W, stirring twice, for 6 minutes.

3. Add the pepper, tomatoes and spices. Cover and cook in their own juices for a further 5 minutes, stirring twice.

4. Add the peas and stir well, cook for a further minute or two then place in a large flat dish to cool.

5. Roll out the pastry and cut out 12 circles 5 inches (12.5 cm) in diameter (you can cut round a large saucer or teaplate). Cut the circles in half.

6. To fill, fold the semicircles round to make a cone, sealing the join by applying gentle pressure as you go.

7. Fill the cone with the meat filling and pinch the open edge to seal. Place on the prepared tray and bake for 3 minutes on High/600W. Glaze and pop under the grill for a couple of minutes to brown, if liked.

Combination cooking Glaze and bake at 400°F/200°C on High/600W for 3 minutes.

Mushroom Flan

Serves 2

Pastry
4 oz (100 g) wholemeal flour
2 oz (50 g) soft vegetable margarine
cold water to mix

Filling
8 oz (225 g) mushrooms
pinch paprika
4 oz (100 g) soft low-fat cheese
4 oz (100 g) Greek-style yoghurt
pinch turmeric

1. Sift the flour into a mixing bowl and rub in the fat until the mixture resembles breadcrumbs in consistency.
2. Bind with enough cold water to make a soft dough, roll out and bake blind in a 6 inch (15 cm) dish.
3. Slice the mushrooms into a dish with a lid and sprinkle with paprika to taste. Cover and cook on High/600W for 2 minutes. Drain off any liquid that is produced.
4. Mix the mushrooms with the cheese, yoghurt and turmeric and place in the baked pastry case. Bake on Medium/360W for 8 minutes.
5. Remove and leave to stand for 5 minutes before serving, if eating hot.

Combination cooking Bake at 375°F/190°C on High/600W for 6 minutes.

Creamy Haddock Flan

Serves 2

Pastry
5 oz (150 g) wholemeal flour
2 oz (50 g) soft vegetable margarine
cold water to mix

Filling
12 oz (300 g) Finnan haddock
8 oz (225 g) natural yoghurt
2 free-range eggs
1 oz (25 g) parmesan cheese
freshly ground black pepper
½ green pepper, diced
1 onion, diced

1. Sift the flour into a mixing bowl and rub in the margarine until the mixture resembles breadcrumbs in consistency.
2. Mix to a soft dough with the water and roll out on a lightly floured board. Bake blind in a 7 inch (17.5 cm) dish.
3. Poach the haddock with just enough water to cover, in a dish with a lid, on Medium/360W for 5 minutes. Leave to stand for 3 minutes.
4. Flake the fish from the skin and bones and liquidize or mash with the yoghurt, eggs, cheese and black pepper to as smooth a consistency as desired for the flan filling.
5. Place the onion and green pepper in a dish with a lid and soften by cooking on High/600W for 4 minutes, stirring once.
6. Stir the vegetables into the fish mixture and pour into the baked case. Return to the oven on Medium/360W for 5 minutes. Stand for 5 minutes and repeat.
7. After cooking you can place under a hot grill for a couple of minutes to colour the top.

Combination cooking Bake at 350°F/180°C on Medium/360W for 7 minutes.

Chicken Pie

Serves 2

Pastry
8 oz (225 g) wholemeal flour
4 oz (100 g) soft vegetable margarine
cold water to mix
egg wash

Filling
6 oz (175 g) chicken, skinless and boneless
1 large onion, diced
4 oz (100 g) mushrooms, sliced
1 tbsp soft vegetable margarine or oil
1 tbsp wholemeal flour
about ⅛ pint (75 ml) skimmed milk

freshly ground black pepper
1 tsp dried parsley

1. Sift the flour into a mixing bowl. Rub in the fat until the mixture resembles breadcrumbs in consistency and bind to a soft dough with the water.
2. Roll out and line a 6 × 4½ inch (15 × 11.5 cm) dish, saving enough pastry to make a lid to the pie.
3. First bake the base blind, then roll out and cut the pastry lid, making it a little bigger than needed because you are also going to bake the lid blind and it will shrink slightly. Bake it blind by placing on a sheet of greaseproof paper and pricking all over with a fork, then cooking on High/600W for 60 seconds.
4. To prepare the filling, place the chicken, onion and mushrooms in a dish with a lid and cook in their own juices on High/600W for 2 minutes. Stir and repeat twice. Remove from the oven and leave to stand while the sauce is made.
5. Place the fat and flour in a jug and mix well. Cook on High/600W for 30 seconds. Remove and stir, adding the juices produced by the cooked meat and vegetables as you do so. Return to the oven for a further 30 seconds on High/600W and then stir again. Add enough milk to make just over ¼ pint (150 ml) liquid and cook and stir as before. Remove and season with freshly ground black pepper and the parsley.
6. Fill the pie with the chicken filling and baste the edges of the pastry lid and pie with egg wash. Place the lid in position and bake on High/600W for 7 minutes.

Combination cooking Glaze and bake at 400°F/200°C on High/600W for 5 minutes.

Tuna Pasties

Makes 4

Yeasted pastry
8 oz (225 g) wholemeal flour
½ oz (12 g) fresh yeast
¼ pint (150 ml) lukewarm water

Filling
1 onion, diced
2 tbsp natural yoghurt
1 free-range egg
7 oz (200 g) can tuna fish
4 tbsp cooked peas

Tuna Pasties (page 98) and Anchovy Pizza (page 86)

1. Sift the flour into a mixing bowl.
2. Crumble the yeast into the water and stir well, then mix into the flour to make a soft dough. Prove on High/600W for 15 seconds, and rest for 10 minutes.
3. Place the onion in a dish with a lid and cook, covered, on High/600W for 2 minutes, stirring once.
4. Add the yoghurt, lightly beaten egg (reserve a little for glazing the pasties), flaked tuna and peas to the onion and mix well.
5. Roll out the yeasted pastry on a lightly floured board and cut out 4 circles of about 5 inches in diameter – use a saucer or small plate as a template.
6. Pile the filling along the centre and glaze the edges with egg, then bring the edges up over the filling, pinching them into an attractive seam. Glaze the pasties.
7. Prove by placing in the oven on High/600W for 15 seconds, then leave to rise in the oven for 15 minutes. After they have risen bake on High/600W for 6 minutes.

Combination cooking Glaze and bake at 375°F/190°C on High/600W for 5 minutes.

Quiche Lorraine

Serves 4

Pastry
8 oz (225 g) wholemeal flour
4 oz (100 g) soft vegetable margarine
skimmed milk to mix

Filling
4 lean back rashers bacon
1 tbsp freshly chopped or 1 tsp dried parsley
1 onion, diced
12 oz (325 g) fromage frais or crème fraîche
3 free-range eggs
freshly ground black pepper

1. Sift the flour into a mixing bowl and rub in the fat until the mixture resembles breadcrumbs in consistency. Stir in the milk to make a soft dough.
2. Roll out on a lightly floured surface and bake blind in a 7 inch (17.5 cm) flan dish.
3. Trim the rind and any fat from the bacon and place in a dish with the parsley and onion. Cover and cook on High/600W for 3 minutes, stirring once.

Stollen (page 104), Hot Cross Buns (page 102) and Peppakakor (page 103)

4. Lightly beat the fromage frais, eggs and black pepper and stir in the cooked bacon and onion.

5. Pour into the prepared pastry case and bake on Medium/360W for 8 minutes, allow to stand for 5 minutes, then continue cooking for a further 4 minutes on Medium/360W.

Combination cooking Bake the filled quiche at 350°F/180°C on Medium/360W for 6 minutes. Stand for 5 minutes before serving.

Herb Cheese Fingers

Makes 12
8 oz (225 g) wholemeal flour
½ oz (12 g) fresh yeast
1 tsp finely chopped fresh mixed herbs
¼ pint (150 ml) lukewarm water
3½ oz (90 g) goat's cheese
a little egg wash or skimmed milk to glaze

1. Sift the flour into a mixing bowl, crumble on the yeast and mix well.
2. Stir in the herbs and then mix in the water to make a soft dough. Knead lightly and roll out to a long rectangle about 12 × 7 inches (30 × 17.5 cm).
3. Soften the cheese by beating or creaming it and place strips of cheese along the length of the rectangle at roughly one-inch intervals. Brush the dough between the strips with egg wash and cut into strips either side of the filling. Fold over to make 'fingers' and cut each finger into four.
4. Seal the ends of the fingers by pressing lightly with a fork to make indentations.
5. Place in the oven and prove on High/600W for 15 seconds, then leave to rise for 10 minutes. Bake on High/600W for 4.30 minutes. Glaze with egg wash or milk and place under the grill to brown lightly, if liked.

Combination cooking Glaze and bake at 400°F/200°C on High/600W for 4 minutes.

CHRISTMAS AND EASTER

CHRISTMAS CAKES and puddings may be lighter in colour when microbaked, but because they will also be lighter in texture they are likely to be much more enjoyable for most people, especially at a time of year when there are many heavy and high-calorie meals.

A microwaved Christmas pudding will not have the dark colour traditionally associated with the long steaming process, but it has a good flavour and as it is light (even though wholemeal flour is used) it will appeal to those who are not so keen on a rich pudding as well as to those who just like Christmas pudding. The recipe here is also free from animal fats and is lower in fat and sugar than many traditional ones. It contains brandy, which will help preserve it, and can be made up to a month before Christmas, but it is best to store the pudding in the fridge.

My family enjoyed the microbaked version and preferred it in many cases to the traditional dark pudding which was tasted alongside it. You can cover the pudding with brandy and serve it flaming in the usual way. It goes particularly well with 'real' custard which is also lower in calories and fat than double cream, while still being delicious and traditional.

As with the pudding, a microbaked Christmas cake will not have the customary dark colour of a rich fruit cake. However, it will still have an excellent flavour. And although microbaked cakes can be drier and stale quickly the Christmas cake can be prepared three or four weeks ahead and stored in an airtight tin in a cool place.

Hot Cross Buns

Makes 12
12 oz (325 g) wholemeal flour
1 tsp mixed spice
¼ tsp turmeric or pinch saffron
2 oz (50 g) currants
2 oz (50 g) mixed peel
1 oz (25 g) unsalted butter
¼ pint (150 ml) skimmed milk
½ oz (12 g) fresh yeast
1 free-range egg
pastry for crosses (optional)
apricot or honey glaze, or egg wash

1. Line a microwave tray.
2. Sift the flour and spices into a mixing bowl and stir in the dried fruit.
3. Place the butter and milk in a jug or basin and melt on Medium/360W for 1.30 minutes. When the mixture is lukewarm, but not hot, crumble in the yeast and mix to a paste.

4. Lightly beat the egg.
5. Make a well in the flour and add the egg, whisking with a fork to combine it with the flour and gradually adding the rest of the liquid at the same time.
6. Lightly knead the dough for a couple of minutes, then prove on High/600W for 15 seconds, cover and stand for 10 minutes.
7. Knock back and shape into rolls. At this stage you can add crosses made from pastry trimmings, or slash crosses in the tops of the buns. Prove on High/600W for 15 seconds, then leave to double in size.
8. Bake in two batches on High/600W for 4.30 minutes. Remove and cool on a wire tray, glazing with apricot jam or honey while hot. If preferred, bake and then glaze with egg wash or milk and brown under the grill.

Combination cooking Glaze with egg wash and bake at 400°F/200°C on High/600W for 4 minutes.

Peppakakor (Swedish Christmas Biscuits)

Makes 24
1 oz (25 g) clear honey
1 oz (25 g) demerara sugar
1 oz (25 g) soft vegetable margarine
3 oz (75 g) wholemeal flour
1 tsp baking powder
¼ tsp each ground ginger, ground cinnamon
pinch ground cloves
2 tbsp skimmed milk
apricot or honey glaze, or egg white

1. Place the honey, sugar and margarine in a jug and warm on Medium/360W for 60 seconds.
2. Sift together the flour, spices and baking powder and stir in the honey mixture.
3. Blend in enough of the milk to make a soft dough and knead very lightly on a floured surface until the dough is ready to roll out thinly.
4. Cut out the biscuits using a small heart-shaped cutter and place half on a lined microwave tray. Bake on High/600W for 3 minutes.
5. Remove from the tray and glaze with honey or apricot jam while cooling on a wire tray. Bake the rest of the biscuits.

Combination cooking Glaze with egg white and bake at 375°F/190°C on High/600W for 3 minutes.

Simnel Cake

Serves 12-14
6 oz (175 g) soft vegetable margarine
4 oz (100 g) dark muscovado sugar
3 free-range eggs (size 2)
8 oz (225 g) wholemeal flour
1 tsp mixed spice
4 oz (100 g) sultanas
4 oz (100 g) currants
4 oz (100 g) raisins
8 oz (225 g) white or raw cane sugar marzipan

1. Beat together the margarine and sugar until light in consistency, pale and creamy.
2. Lightly beat the eggs and add to the margarine.
3. Sift the flour and mixed spice and fold into the cake mixture.
4. Stir in the dried fruit.
5. Place half the cake mixture in the base of a lined 7 inch (17.5 cm) cake dish.
6. Place the marzipan in the microwave (unwrapped if it is in a metallic wrapper) and soften on High/600W for 15 seconds. Roll out on a lightly floured board into two 7 inch (17.5 cm) circles.
7. Place one of the circles on top of the cake mixture in the dish, cover with the rest of the cake mixture, then place the second circle of marzipan on top.
8. Bake on High/600W for 8 minutes, turning three times. Remove from the oven and stand for 5 minutes, then carefully invert on to a wire cooling tray covered with a sheet of greaseproof paper to prevent the marzipan top from being marked. Quickly peel off the paper lining and reinvert on to a second tray. Leave until completely cold.

Combination cooking Bake at 350°F/180°C on Medium/360W for 10 minutes, followed by a further 4 minutes on conventional heat only.

Stollen

Serves 10
½ oz (12 g) fresh yeast
⅛ pint (75 ml) water
2 oz (50 g) soft vegetable margarine
⅛ pint (75 ml) skimmed milk
2 oz (50 g) clear honey
8 oz (225 g) wholemeal flour
2 oz (50 g) raisins

1 oz (25 g) mixed peel
2 oz (50 g) walnut pieces
1 free-range egg
fruit glacé icing

1. Lightly oil a savarin mould or microwave ring dish.
2. Measure the water into a jug and heat on High/600W for 10 seconds.
Remove and crumble in the yeast.
3. Place the margarine, milk and honey in a second jug and melt on
High/600W for 60 seconds.
4. Sift the flour into a mixing bowl and stir in the raisins, peel and walnut
pieces.
5. Lightly beat the egg and then stir it, the milk mixture and the yeast
mixture into the flour. Prove on High/600W for 15 seconds and rest for 15
minutes.
6. Remove from the mixing bowl and lightly knead on a floured surface.
Shape into a sausage and place in the mould. Return to the oven and
prove twice, as before but resting for only 10 minutes. The mixture should
be two-thirds of the way up the sides of the mould.
7. Bake on High/600W for 6 minutes. Take out of the oven and stand in
the dish for 5 minutes, then remove and cool on a wire tray. Drizzle the
icing over the stollen while cooling.

Combination cooking Glaze with egg white and bake at 400°F/200°C
on Medium/360W for 10 minutes. Ice while cooling.

Carob Yule Log

Serves 6

Sponge
3 free-range eggs
3 oz (75 g) dark muscovado sugar
2 oz (50 g) plain carob bar
2 tbsp decaffeinated coffee
2 oz (50 g) wholemeal flour

Filling
4 oz (100 g) low-fat curd cheese
4 oz (100 g) plain carob bar
1 tbsp decaffeinated coffee
1 tsp ground cinnamon

1. Make a paper Swiss roll case by lining a Swiss roll tin 11 × 7 inches
(27.5 × 17.5 cm) with a double layer of greaseproof, baking or silicone
baking paper. Shape the edges by cutting into the corners with scissors and

then folding the edges around. Staple in place at each corner and then strengthen the edges with a layer of brown tape or masking tape. Lightly oil.

2. Whisk together the eggs and sugar until light in colour and thick and ropy in consistency – the mixture should support your initials when written on the top.

3. Melt the carob with the coffee in a dish on High/600W for 60 seconds and fold into the mixture.

4. Sift the flour and carefully fold this in also, retaining as much air as possible.

5. Pour into the prepared case and bake on High/600W for 4.30 minutes or until the sides are coming away from the paper. (Do not worry if the cake is a little moist – it will dry out as it stands, and can also be patted with absorbent kitchen paper to remove any excess moisture after standing for 5 minutes.)

6. Invert the cake on to a clean sheet of greaseproof paper. Trim the edges and roll up with the paper inside.

7. To make the filling, place the cheese in a mixing bowl.

8. Melt the carob with the coffee in a dish on High/600W for 60 seconds, stir into the cheese and add the cinnamon.

9. Carefully unroll the cake, spread with the carob cream, and roll up again. Decorate, if liked, with springs of holly and dust with a little sifted icing sugar.

Combination cooking   Bake at 350°F/180°C on Medium/360W for 5 minutes.

Christmas Pudding

Serves 6-8
2 oz (50 g) soft vegetable margarine
2 oz (50 g) dark muscovado sugar
2 free-range eggs
2 oz (50 g) wholemeal flour
½ tsp each mixed spice and ground ginger
2 oz (50 g) each sultanas, currants and raisins
½ oz (12 g) mixed chopped peel
2 oz (50 g) wholemeal breadcrumbs
2 oz (50 g) finely chopped almonds
3 tbsp brandy
1 tbsp maple syrup or date syrup or molasses

1. Lightly oil a 1½ pint (900 ml) pudding basin.

2. Cream together the margarine and sugar and lightly beat in the eggs.

3. Sift the flour and spices, then mix in the dried fruit and stir in the breadcrumbs and the almonds.

4. Combine the dry and wet ingredients, making the mixture softer by adding the brandy and syrup.
5. Place in the prepared pudding basin and cover the top with a double layer of greaseproof paper tied in place with string.
6. Bake on Medium/360W for 10 minutes.
7. Allow to become completely cold and then change the paper and store for up to a month, preferably in the fridge, until required.
8. Reheat on High/600W for 2-3 minutes.

Combination cooking Bake at 350°F/190°C on Medium/360W for 10 minutes.

Christmas Cake

Serves 16
6 oz (175 g) vegetable margarine
6 oz (175 g) clear honey
4 free-range eggs
4 oz (100 g) each raisins, sultanas, currants
2 oz (50 g) mixed chopped peel
2 oz (50 g) chopped glacé cherries
2 oz (50 g) finely chopped almonds
6 oz (175 g) wholemeal flour
4 oz (100 g) ground almonds
3 tbsp brandy

1. Line a large 7 inch (17.5 cm) cake dish, or a 2½ pint (1.25 litre) soufflé dish, with a double layer of greaseproof paper and oil lightly.
2. Cream together the margarine and honey and beat in the lightly whisked eggs, one at a time and beating well between additions. Add a little flour if the mixture shows signs of curdling.
3. Prepare all the dried fruit and nuts and sift the flour into a mixing bowl. Stir the fruit and nuts into the flour.
4. Fold the flour into the creamed mixture and then stir in the brandy, combining all the ingredients well.
5. Place in the prepared dish and bake on High/600W for 10 minutes, then reduce the power to Medium/360W for a further 10 minutes. Allow to stand for 5 minutes, and if the cake is still moist in the centre when tested by inserting a skewer, bake for a further 3 minutes on Medium/360W.
6. Allow to become completely cold before removing and storing in an airtight tin, wrapped in greaseproof paper inside a layer of aluminium foil.

Combination cooking Bake at 350°F/180°C on Medium/360W for 20 minutes. Allow to stand for 5 minutes, and if the centre is still a little moist return to the oven for a further 1-2 minutes.

Index